ALTERNATE VIEWS, ALTERNATE UNIVERSES

THE ART OF
DAVID B. MATTINGLY

Paper Tiger
An imprint of Dragon's World Ltd
Limpsfield
Surrey RH8 0DY
Great Britain

First published by Dragon's World Ltd, 1996

ISBN 1 85028 340 0 (Limpback)

Art Director John Strange
Editorial Director Pippa Rubinstein

Printed in Singapore

ALTERNATE VIEWS, ALTERNATE UNIVERSES
THE ART OF DAVID B. MATTINGLY

Text by David B. Mattingly with Cathleen Cogswell

For my father,
John W. Mattingly,
artist and scientist,
who showed me it all.

INTRODUCTION

DAVID MATTINGLY: Casting Spells from the Palette of Miracles

In another century, Dave Mattingly would be burned at the stake.

Most people, even artists, simply don't have the kind of visions he has – unless they've tapped a pipeline to Purgatory. Never mind that the Mattingly quarters are swarming with cats (he swears that none of them are familiars!), there is a nova-intensity wave of visual wizardry emanating from his studio. Dante, eat your heart out!

I met Dave in his earliest incarnation, when he laboured as a matte painter at the Disney studios (a place well established on the Map of Magical Kingdoms), long before his work spread across fantasy paperback racks like an enchanted rainbow on a Hyborian battlefield. At the time it probably would not have been unreasonable to qualify him as the sorcerer's apprentice (studying under the illustrious Harrison Ellenshaw), because he wielded a paint brush like a magic wand, creating vistas so lifelike they looked more convincing on screen than the real thing. How he got that skilled so early, only his fairy godmother knows!

One need not look too deeply into his artistic crystal ball to divine his prime inspirations. He was not shaped by the traditional school of American illustrators: Rockwell, Leyendecker, Lovell, von Schmidt, Parker, Cornwell, Falter. His creative roots are grounded less in commercial art than in the imaginative worldscapes of such comic artists as Wood, Williamson and Kirby, in addition to filmmakers like Lang, Menzies, Wise, Allen and Harryhausen. If there is a secret to his success, it could probably be traced to their mythic achievements.

Mattingly has extended the fantastic traditions these artists began in their chosen mediums, which perhaps explains why his work generates a certain resonance. Their images of forgotten civilizations, alien encounters, mad scientists, lost cities, bizarre monsters, futuristic colonies, robot slaves, galactic warfare, atomic mutations, time travellers, architectural utopias, legendary goddesses and sun-bronzed heroes have all become major elements in his evolutionary tapestry of wonder.

Like Paul, Frazetta, Emshwiller and Whelan, Mattingly has found a way to make it all his own. His work is often dominated by geometric shapes: stark horizontals, schematic verticals, tangental arcs, orbiting spheres. He most often paints with a full palette, detouring the safety of limited colour expression, and almost always utilizing primary hues. Another dead tip-off is that he never dodges rendering clusters of complex detail, which many illustrators simply suggest with a few abstract brush strokes. Foreground, middleground and background are all handled with the same focused attention: a distant rebel destroyer executing an Immelmann around an armoured alien asteroid will always be as tight as the colonial cruiser passing just above the viewer – and should anyone bother to look into the cockpit of the far-away warship, more often than not the pilot will be so well defined you could count the buttons on his jacket, maybe even read his rank off the shoulder patch!

Shortcuts are not in David Mattingly's arsenal of painting tricks.

Hardware, however, is on his speciality list, and his skill at rendering realistic machinery is second to none, particularly the massive galactic warships in his space extravaganzas.

My favourite Mattingly spectacular is his Flying High image – a trio of speed jockeys racing above the Arizona desert on chrome anti-grev cycles – which I had the privilege of running as a double-page spread in my pop-culture publication MEDIASCENE (now PREVUE). The scene sums up the essence of Dave Mattingly's magic: a breathtaking vista rendered to Ektachrome perfection; an astonishing vehicle so well designed that there is no doubt about its capability to become airborne; and the young, hellraising rider, a high-tech Icarus skyrocketing across the heavens with breathtaking exhilaration.

The spell Mattingly casts over us, however, is predicated on much more than the ability to capture images with Polaroid-like precision. His work is inevitably cloaked in a certain kind of youthful, naïve charm – with a purity not unlike that of a dream – which gives even his most outrageous paintings an instant accessibility to viewers. It is a special kind of enchantment that can never be learned in a classroom textbook. Unless you are born with it, perhaps the only way to get it is if Merlin materializes on your drawing board and conjures the magic into your soul.

I'm not sure how Mattingly got it. All I know is that if he did what he does in another century, he'd be burned at the stake.

Well, there's still time.

JAMES STERANKO
July 1995

BEGINNINGS

Imagine this scene from a 1960s TV sit-com: mother and father are sitting side-by-side on the couch. Dad wears a suit and tie, and mom, although a housewife, is perfectly coiffeured. Standing to attention before them is a wholesome, freckled-faced boy of ten.

'Well son, what do you want to be when you grow up?'

'A science fiction and fantasy artist.'

As the parents faint, dad keeling forward, mom wilting into a heap, the screen blackens and then discreetly switches to an advertisement.

When I play that scene in my mind, I realize how fortunate I've been to have understanding and encouraging parents. As a child, they made me feel I could do anything I wanted to with my life, and gave me free rein to develop my artistic abilities. While less tolerant folks might have discouraged such a path, mine allowed me to pursue my dream.

I was born in 1956 in Fort Collins, a small town in Colorado. It was a wonderful place to grow up. The world was more innocent then. No one had to lock their doors. My friends and I would get on our bicycles and disappear for hours at a time, and none of our parents worried. I was a normal child in all aspects but one – from a very young age, I knew I wanted to be an artist.

I was christened David Burroughs Mattingly, after the neoclassical painter Jacques Louis David and writer Edgar Rice Burroughs. From that choice of names, it seems inevitable that I would become a science fiction and fantasy artist. Among my earliest memories are those of lying in front of our big fireplace as my mother read aloud the Burroughs *Tarzan* and *Mars* books. As I stared into the fire, I would vividly imagine the scenes my mother described. Around the age of three, I was given my first box of crayons and the world became my canvas – quite literally – and for a while, nothing in the house was safe from my youthful graffiti. This was an easier stage for my mother to manage than when, at age five, I melted crayons, à la Jackson Pollock, on the heating ducts.

Throughout grade school, I drew constantly and was an omnivorous reader of comic books, qualities shared with my two best pals. We formed a pint-sized art group, and were in fierce rivalry to draw the best comic books, featuring such characters as *The Rebel, Holden Tempest*, and *Thunderclap*, the man who could cause earthquakes by smashing his hands together. Throughout my formative years, I persisted in the thought that I would become a comic book artist. It was only after I got to art school that I found my talents lay more in painting.

I went away to The Principia, a prep school in St. Louis, Missouri, for the first two and a half years of high school, but was kicked out for bad behaviour. I attended the rest of high school in Ft Collins, where although salutatorian of my class, I remained something of a rebel. I had an underground comic strip, entitled *Radic the Destroyer*, and on the sly substituted all the photos of me in the senior year book with Edvard Munch-like screaming self-portraits.

After graduation, I went to Colorado Institute of Art in Denver for a year, and also took classes at Colorado State University in the film department because of a budding interest in movie special effects. Feeling I still wasn't getting the education I needed, I transferred to Art Center College of Design in Pasadena, California. I credit the preparation I got there for making me a professional. One teacher in particular, noted illustrator Barron Storey, inspired me and showed me that art is a continuous process of discovery – there is always something new to learn and master.

At Art Center, I lived at the Golden Palm, a rather dilapidated apartment complex that had seen better days, but attracted art students with its cheap rents. The Golden Palm has been the home to a surprising number of creative artists. I was roommate with Paul Chadwick, creator of the comic book *Concrete*, who is still my best friend. Others in the Golden Palm orbit included science fiction illustrators Alan Gutierrez, Bryn Barnard, Richard Hescox, *Dinotopia* author James Gurney, *The Mask* and *Time Cop* screenwriter Mark Verheiden, cartoonist Ron Harris, and Tom Kinkaid, who promotes himself as *The Painter of Light* in his infommercials.

While still attending Art Center, I got a job designing a film for producer Howard Ziehm. He wanted to make a sequel to his hugely successful (and rather raunchy) parody, *Flesh Gordon*. I did thirty paintings, two of which are included here (see page 10). It was a fascinating introduction to filmmaking. Howard had several films in various stages of completion, so while working on the project I was able to observe all aspects of film production and editing, and became interested in matte painting – an optical process that combines live action film with painting. A typical example of a matte painting is this: a director needs a shot of a character walking up to a huge futuristic city encapsulated in a glass dome. Using movie 'magic,' the character is photographed walking up to one small section of the city that has been mocked up on a set, and the matte artist paints in the rest. The two elements are then combined optically.

Becoming a matte artist was a way to combine my interest in film and painting. I borrowed the paintings I did for *Flesh Gordon*, took them around

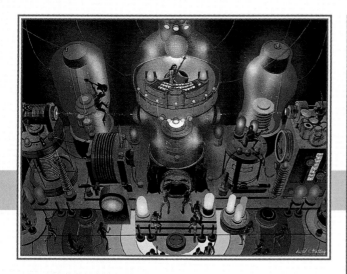

Production design paintings for the
sequel to **Flesh Gordon** (1978)

to various film studios, and got several job offers. I chose Walt Disney Studios for the opportunity to work under Harrison Ellenshaw, who headed the matte department and has gone on to become a vice president in charge of the special effects branch of the studio, Buena Vista Visual Effects. Harrison became my mentor, and taught me everything I know about the craft.

I stayed at Walt Disney for 5 years, working on *The Return of the Apple Dumpling Gang, The Devil and Max Devlin, Herbie Goes Bananas, The Black Hole, Tron, A Watcher in the Woods,* and many other instant classics. At age 23, I became a full matte artist, the youngest so designated in the history of the industry, I was told. When Harrison Ellenshaw left Disney to set up the Industrial Light and Magic matte department, I was tapped as his successor, becoming the youngest department head at the studio.

Even though most of my work today is as a book cover artist, I occasionally accept projects as a matte artist. I took three months off to work on Warren Beatty's *Dick Tracy*, painting much of the opening panoramic shot seen at the bottom of this page. I have done mattes for television commercials, promoting such diverse products as chemical fertilizers and personal banking services. Most recently, I contributed matte paintings to two Stephen King TV mini-series, *The Stand* and *The Langoliers*.

While still working at Disney, I sent out samples of my work to publishers to get cover assignments. My first published work was *Call for the Dead* (see page 9) for *The Magazine of Fantasy and Science Fiction*. My first paperback book assignment, *A Wizard in Bedlam* (*see* right) came from the late Don Wollheim at DAW Books. I can

still remember the day I got the proof of that cover in the mail. Seeing my first printed cover was an indescribable thrill. I'll never forget it, nor will my first wife, Barbara, who witnessed my impromptu dance around the living room, cover raised over my head like a trophy.

I was doing eight or ten covers a year while still working at Disney, but I felt torn between freelance work and my duties at the studio. I loved working with the people at Disney, but I knew I had to choose which field would have priority in my life. People have since asked how I could leave such a secure position for the vagaries of the life of a freelance illustrator, and the answer is the help and encouragement of the legendary editor, Judy Lynn Del Rey, who persuaded me to move to New York in 1983.

I was under contract to her company, Ballantine/Del Rey Books, for the first two years after the move, so she provided the safety net I needed. I have been happy as a freelancer ever since. It gives me the luxury of working on a wide variety of projects for different clients. I have done covers for literally every major publisher of science fiction and fantasy including Ace, Avon, Baen, Bantam, Berkley, Dell, Roc, Signet, and Tor Books; and several that have gone out of business (through no fault of my own) including Playboy and Pageant Books. After living in a TriBeCa loft in New York City for my first year, I moved across the Hudson River to Hoboken, New Jersey, which has one of the best unobstructed views of the Manhattan skyline. I have resided here for the last twelve years, and now live with my second wife, Cathleen Cogswell, and our three cats, Mouse, Buster and Orphan Annie.

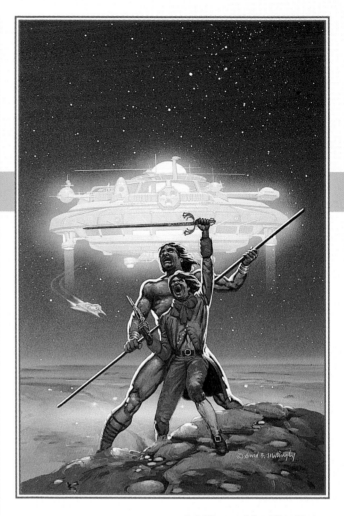

A Wizard in Bedlam
(DAW Books, 1979)

Opening panorama from **Dick Tracy**
(Used by permission from The Walt Disney Company, 1990)

11

VISIONS OF THE FUTURE

What will the future be like? Like Rorschach blots, the answers are self-revealing. Pessimists envision a totalitarian world government, an environmental holocaust, or machines taking over the earth and enslaving their former masters. Optimists imagine a futuristic Utopia: science will conquer disease, poverty, hunger; man will overcome his baser nature and war will be a thing of the past.

Trying to predict how the world will turn out is a game of luck and skill. The more one knows about the rules of probability, the better one plays, which is why some of the world's greatest minds, many of them scientists by profession, have produced some monumental fiction exploring what theoretically could happen in the future. In my opinion, the best science fiction extrapolates from what we know to be true, and what might be true *if* our scientific knowledge and capabilities were more advanced.

I suspect that Ridley Scott's movie *Bladerunner* probably got it visually right: a world of huge technological marvels for those at the top, and extreme poverty for the rest of humanity. That does seem to be the direction in which this information age is heading. But then, who really knows? Think of how drastically the world has changed in the last hundred years. What discoveries will come along in the next century that will irrevocably change the path of humanity? Communication with extraterrestrials? Antigravity? Faster-than-light travel? Life after death?

This is where the artist humbly makes an entrance. The science fiction and fantasy cover artist interprets the writer's conception, giving words visual dimension and shape. One of the artists whose positive vision of the future has given me inspiration is Robert McCall. Around the time I got the assignment to do the cover for *The Rapture Effect*, I heard that McCall had been stricken with a heart attack. The book has some very McCall like elements in it, so I decided to make *The Rapture Effect* a homage to him, in gratitude for the great paintings he has done. Even though our styles are distinctly different, there are elements in this painting that make reference to his work. I should mention that I ran into McCall and his wife at the Canaletto show at the Metropolitan Museum of Art, and he was fully recovered.

I wanted *The Rapture Effect* to show what it would feel like to be inside a computer, depicted as a vast netscape of interconnecting electronic circuits. The background is patterned like a microchip, but at the same time, conveys the feeling of a starscape, intermixing the infinitely small universe of microchip technology and the infinite depths of space.

Halo and *Ark Liberty* both use a mixed-media technique that achieves wonderful results. I wet the canvas, spray enamel paint on to the water surface, and then re-spray the water, which breaks the enamel into interesting fractured patterns. The technique is particularly evident in the coral in *Ark Liberty,* and in the space background in *Halo*.

I was assigned the cover for James Blish's classic book, *Cities in Flight* (see pages 16-17) right after I returned from working on Warren Beatty's *Dick Tracy*. The motion picture had a strong, highly-stylized production design: all the costumes, sets and matte paintings were in bright primary colours. Although the film got a lukewarm critical reception, it was an Oscar nominee for Best Art Direction. I thought it pulled off the difficult task of finding the celluloid equivalent of a Sunday newspaper's comics page. I'm proud of what I did on the picture as part of a talented team. While painting is a solitary pursuit, films are an amazing hive of activity. In the Disney matte department, there is a genuine sense of camaraderie and pooled effort.

The buildings in the central bubble in *Cities in Flight* are done in a Dick Tracy style, and the whole painting has a directness and freshness that came from working at the studio with other matte artists. I tend to plan my paintings carefully, and once I have a complete drawing, I usually don't deviate from it much. Under Harrison Ellenshaw's direction at Disney, there was a lot of emphasis on keeping the painting loose as you blocked it in, making changes as they occurred to you and not being afraid to try new things. I still remember watching Harrison's father, Peter Ellenshaw, work on a matte. If he got a better idea and decided to repaint a section of the sky, he would dive right in, painting over anything that got in his way. I would have masked out the foreground elements so that I wouldn't lose any of my careful work. The Ellenshaws have had a good effect on me. While I still tend to be methodical in my approach, I am willing to take bigger chances on the fly.

In the case of *Cities in Flight*, publisher Jim Baen had a tight deadline, and gave me free rein. He didn't even request a sketch. I did a quick rough for myself and then started to paint, letting inspiration be my guide. I sketched directly on the canvas with a brush, pushing globs of paint around until the masses looked right. I went in with the airbrush only to blend the tones at the very end, softening the nebula and adding the glows. It's an exhilarating, if chancy, way to paint.

© MATTINGLY 90

The Changes
(Dell Books, 1991)

The Changes and The World Next Door are two apocalyptic visions of the future. The Changes is the first cover for a trilogy about a future in which people suddenly develop a phobia about technology, and leave the cities. I illustrated the obvious scene, the mass exodus, but getting the reference turned into something of a Crocodile Dundee adventure.

I needed to get shots of a crush of people walking toward me from a very high angle. I borrowed an 18ft ladder from New York photographer Addie Passen, and set it up in the middle of the sidewalk on Broadway, a major pedestrian thoroughfare in Manhattan. I then perched on the top of the ladder with my camera, and started to shoot interesting looking people to be featured in the painting. Unfortunately, some people in Manhattan take offense at having strangers shoot their picture, so after a few angry altercations, I switched tactics. I pretended to be shooting pictures of the surrounding architecture, and acted annoyed every time I caught someone in the frame; naturally, I was careful to shoot first and then wave them out of the way. I particularly like the two old women in the middle ground, the one with a cane and shopping bag, and the other in the plaid yellow coat. They were among the people who strayed into my viewfinder, and I used them exactly as they appeared without changing a detail. Addie Passen, who loaned me the ladder, is the lady with two shopping bags and a hat on the right.

The World Next Door is an alternate universe novel where there is a nuclear exchange at the time of the Cuban missile crisis in the 1960s. A pathway develops between two universes, one destroyed by a nuclear exchange, and one where the world crisis is averted and people live in peace. Some people in the devastated world are able to escape through the portal to safety. I love to play warm colours against cool colours, and this was the perfect opportunity. I used hot colours for the war-ravaged world, and cool colours for the serene world. I put a red dress on the girl in the cool world because it draws your eye to that spot, pulling you through the chaos to the greenery and mountains beyond.

I have to admit I enjoyed painting the mushroom cloud of the atomic explosion. What a strange dichotomy – a force of such power and beauty, that is the ultimate weapon of destruction, frightening and awesome as the power of the sun unleashed on earth.

© MATTINGLY 90

The World Next Door
(Tor Books, 1990)

The Kalif's War
(Baen Books, 1990)

The covers for *The Kalif's War* and *The Crystal Empire* are both wrap-arounds, or paintings that extend from front to back covers of a book. This design presents a different set of challenges and rewards from a normal front cover painting. To begin with, the canvas is twice as large. On a wrap-around cover, the main subject must fit into the lower half to two-thirds of the front cover, to allow for the title and author's name in the upper region. The second part of the painting, which will run on the back cover, cannot have anything too important or contrasting on it, since much of the design will be buried under type. In planning the design, you must allow room for the UPC seal, a big white square that takes up about an eighth of the back cover. So for all practical purposes, the only area that will be seen without type or other design elements on top of it is the lower two-thirds of the right side. An illustrator is at the mercy of the book designer who decides where all the type will go. Most times the type is carefully placed so that important parts of the illustration are preserved, but not always.

Even with these restrictions, I still enjoy doing wrap-arounds because they allow me to work large – creating a panoramic view of the book's world. And it is not as if all of my painstaking detail work on the back is for naught. I still have the original painting, sans type, to display or sell.

The covers for the Realtime books were originally done by artist Thomas Kidd. When I did the cover for an omnibus collection of the stories, I liked what he had done so much that I put small, spherical versions of two of his covers in my painting for *Across Realtime* (see pages 22–3) and signed it 'David T.K. Mattingly'.

The Crystal Empire
(Tor Books, 1985)

21

The Pellucidar Series

Having a chance to do Edgar Rice Burroughs' Pellucidar series was a dream come true. I grew up on Burroughs' books, which fired my early interest in fantasy and science fiction. Also, two of my idols, fantasy artists Frank Frazetta and Roy Krenkel, had done inspired covers for the series. I was initially intimidated by the prospect of coming up against such great artists, since I knew comparisons of my interpretation to theirs was inevitable. After several dozen sketches, and a lot of thought, I arrived at a unique solution, one that I felt I could call my own. I decided to paint a giant panorama of

Pellucidar
(Ballantine Books, 1990)

the Pellucidar landscape, with the six paintings joining end-to-end like a hinged, multi-panelled Japanese screen. The first and last paintings join also, so the work actually forms a continuous loop.

Unfortunately, the designer at Ballantine Books who was in charge of the project and is now no longer with the company, decided to disregard my careful planning. He boxed the paintings on the covers so that it was impossible to line them up on the shelf to form one long design.

Here, the covers are presented in the large format, and if you are willing to buy two additional

© MATTINGLY 89

copies of this book you can lay them side by side and see the grand design I intended.

I usually do one and a half paintings a month. This rate allows me to maintain the quality of my work. For the Pellucidar series, the pace wildly accelerated. For scheduling reasons I had to pro-

duce a completed painting roughly every six days. I felt like a ten-minute-mile jogger on a berserk treadmill going four times that speed. For the entire month and a half I had for the project, I worked eighteen-hour days, and ended with a gruelling race to the finish   a seventy-two-hour

© MATTINGLY 89

non-stop painting marathon to polish off *Savage Pellucidar*. I hate working on that sort of schedule because it rarely produces the kind of work I'm happy with. This project was so important to me, however, that I gritted my teeth and did it anyway.

The model for the first painting, *At the Earth's Core*, is Fabio, who has gone on to be quite a media star. He used to model in New York and was in great demand because of his incredible musculature and long hair. I often use the Manhattan photographer Addie Passen to shoot reference photographs. Addie has an all female staff, and

Land of Terror
(Ballantine Books, 1990)

they turned to jelly when Fabio came in. That was a pretty good indication that he was going on to bigger things. I've used a lot of top models before and after that, and I've never seen the staff react to anyone that way again. Fabio was a trooper. He was always cooperative, held difficult poses with-

out complaint and good-naturedly wore the crazy costumes the scenes required.

Although I never met Roy Krenkel, I closely followed his career, and feel a real bond with him because of his art. His work has been overshadowed by his friend Frank Frazetta's

28

Savage Pellucidar
(Ballantine Books, 1990)

because Krenkel was less flashy and his figure work never as dynamic (but then, is anyone's figure work as dynamic as Frazetta's?). But Krenkel was a visionary, and every one of his paintings and drawings exudes a depth of knowledge of his subject. If I ever get to visit Pellucidar, I'm sure it will look just like Krenkel painted it. Roy was the spiritual model for the old man, Abner Perry, on the cover for *Savage Pellucidar*. It is not an exact likeness, as Roy didn't have a moustache, but I tried to capture his incredible pluck and *joie de vivre*.

FUNNY STUFF

Humour can be a lot like politics – what one person thinks is great, another may dismiss as stupid. And with both, you also have to worry about being politically correct. Sometimes it seems that in America's melting-pot culture, everything is off limits. When I hired an American Indian to pose for *Aquila and the Sphinx* (see page 32), he refused to assume the pose in the approved sketch, because he thought it stereotypical. Only after working out a mutually acceptable position were we able to get on with the shoot. I also had a professional female model get irked because I wanted her to pose for *Back to the Stone Age* (see page 27), with only her long blonde hair covering her breasts. I thought that this had been pre-arranged by the photographer, but there had been a mix-up. After half an hour of haggling, I shot her in a halter top and then used my wife for the torso. Cathleen didn't mind of course, but then, we are on more intimate terms.

Humour, in its simplest and most direct form, has universal appeal, and that's what I strive for. Children and adults alike will snicker at the sight of a dignified man losing his hat to the wind and chasing it wildly down the street, or an animal performing a stupid trick. In art as well, the comic often comes from exaggeration: overblown reactions, a skewed perspective on the commonplace, sight gags.

I am probably not the first artist an art director thinks of when they get a book needing a funny cover, but I love to do them and actively seek such assignments. Rather than making the characters look funny through distortion, I prefer to let the humour come from the situation. For instance, it is funny to see strange creatures displaying human-like behaviour, like the *Harpy High* monsters in the locker room (see page 37) or the fairytale characters sitting on the stoop eating ice cream cones in *Land Of Laughs* (see page 39). I also like to sprinkle comic details throughout my paintings to reward those who take the time to study them.

In *Ever After*, I hope people will notice some of its subtler elements, such as how the caped prince playing poker with the dragon wears an odd smile. The reason becomes apparent if you notice the cards in his hand; he's holding a royal flush. One also can assume from the dragon's treasure hoard that this is a high-stakes game. I put some unusual pieces in with the booty, such as the *Venus de Milo* from the Louvre's collection, and another inestimable masterpiece, my painting, *The Subway Wizard*.

I was an omnivorous reader of *Mad* magazine as a youngster, and the release of a new issue was a highlight of the month. A friend, who was an early comic collector, gave me access to the earliest issues of *Mad*, which contained much of Wally Wood's greatest humorous work. Wood and Jack Davis were my favourite *Mad* artists as a child, and, come to think of it, they still are. While revisiting childhood terrain is often disappointing, their work remains fresh and funny to me even today.

Wood did hilarious things with background detail – kooky little figures, and signs with running gags. I would scrutinize each panel for fear of missing some sly little treasure. I think this is what fuelled my tendency to weave inside jokes into my paintings. I know I am guilty sometimes of doing it to excess (see *The Wizard of Sunset Strip* on page 72, or *The Nine Lives of Catseye Gomez* on page 38), but I get a kick out of it.

The Aquiliad and *Aquila and the Sphinx* both show the influence of those two zany artists. *The Aquiliad* typifies my idea of a *Mad* set-up, and might be entitled *The Food Chain* – our hero in the foreground, eating with visible gusto, is totally oblivious to the fact he is about to become a main course himself.

When I am trying to get a hand on what a character looks like, I often draw on a public figure, actor, or someone I know as a visual substitute. That way, as I am doing the sketches, I have a mental model on which to pattern a character's facial expressions, posture, gestures and attitudes. For instance, in *Aquila and the Sphinx*, I thought of Tonto in a toga. In the case of *Codgerspace* (see page 34), I thought of the great matte painter Peter Ellenshaw, a spry Englishman with a contagious enthusiasm for painting. Although Peter didn't pose for this piece, my visual memory was strong enough that I was able to capture what I needed of his character.

I think one of the reasons I was able to become an artist is because of this visual memory. My wife Cathleen is a writer, and her memory functions in a completely different way from mine. I remember things in pictures; she remembers things in words. For instance, if we go to the movies and one of our friends asks what happened in it, Cathe can recount the plot in great detail. I don't remember the ins and outs of the plot, but I can tell about the look and feel of the picture, including detailed descriptions of shots I thought were particularly good. The same holds true when I read books – I think in pictures, not in terms of plot, which is why I enjoy visual writers so much.

Aquila and the Sphinx
(Del Rey Books, 1987)

The Aquiliad
(Del Rey Books, 1986)

© MATTINGLY 91

Unicorn U
(Ace Books, 1991)

Unicorn U and Harpy High are covers for two extremely funny books by Esther Friesner. I met Esther at a science fiction convention, and was struck by her bubbly, blond looks, so when I needed a cheerleader for Unicorn U, I had to look no further than the author herself. I called Esther and floated the idea. She good–naturedly agreed and borrowed her teenage daughter's pom-poms, then had her husband photograph her doing a series of cheers. Esther is the fair–haired cheerleader on the left, with the monster looking up her skirt.

There are two other notable cameo appearances in this painting. One by Concrete, my friend Paul Chadwick's comic character, and the other by my beautiful wife Cathleen, who for once was not turned into a monster or wizard. She is Esther's dark–haired complement.

I put a lot of work into the little comic details in Harpy High. Take special note of the pin-up in the open locker behind the green-scaled monster. It is a female of the same species, with suitably hefty proportions, striking a Marilyn Monroe pose. And yes, the fur ball with the hockey stick was inspired by Critters, a hilarious low–budget science fiction flick.

Doing a cover for an author's work is a creative collaboration, but more often than not, the artist and author never speak directly, let alone meet.

That is why it is such a treat to be assigned multiple books by the same author, especially when the writing is as appealing as Friesner's. She makes me laugh out loud, and her books abound with zany images.

The Nine Lives of Catseye Gomez (see page 38), is another painting with subtle background jokes. There are multiple copies of a poster on the wall for a musical group called 'Barclay and the Hose Heads', a reference to friend and fellow artist Barclay Shaw who dabbles in music. Notice the human hand sticking out of the garbage can. Also in the garbage is a copy of Catseye author Simon Hawke's novel, The Wizard of 4th Street. The sign in the background says 'Gnemos', a little plug for fellow artist Thomas Kidd's upcoming book. There are many more, but the others you will have to figure out for yourself.

The story in Land of Laughs (see page 39), starts out humorous and light, but turns terribly dark half-way through. I wanted to show this change of tone in my cover illustration. The sinister figure in the window foreshadows the unhappy events that will destroy the idyllic scene on the front porch. The dogs are inspired by the work of cartoonist George Booth, who draws wonderfully grizzled dogs and cats.

The Nine Lives of Catseye Gomez
(Questar Books, 1992)

Majyk by Hook or Crook
(Ace Books, 1993)

Majyk by Design
(Ace Books, 1994)

The illustrations for *Majyk by Accident* and *Majyk by Design* are take-offs of romance covers. While romances are not to my literary taste, I admire many of the artists who work in the genre. For one thing, they are masters at painting skin tones, which is fortunate, since there tends to be a lot of bare chest and décolletage. I also admire the interesting compositions that the more adventurous artists use. The covers follow a locked-in formula: basically, a couple in passionate embrace. It takes real creativity to come up with a new angle on that.

For the cover of *Majyk by Accident*, I observed the conventions of romance cover art, from the bright pastel colour scheme to the oversized flowers growing out of nowhere. However, there is a deviation from the norm. The soulful embrace is interrupted by a boy chasing a magical cat through a dimensional portal.

All three of the *Majyk* covers feature cats, and since we have three felines as pets, you would think I would have plenty of access to whiskered models. Think again. Cats are very independent creatures to begin with, and unlike dogs, never repeat a trick on command. Our three carry this trait to the extreme, refusing to hold still for even the few seconds it takes to aim and snap a picture. In this series, I had to get my material from reference books containing cat photos, and patch together the pose I needed.

Most of our cats were wild strays who adopted us. While feral cats make wonderful pets, they are never completely socialized. Mouse, a beautiful white cat with a gray cap, was badly mistreated before we rescued her. She still hides in the closet whenever anyone visits, and amazingly, reappears the second they leave. Some of our close friends joke that Mouse is just a figment of our imagination, since they've never caught so much as a glimpse of her. The pose in *Majyk by Hook or Crook* was inspired by Mouse. Every night when my wife and I watch the news, Mouse jumps up on the couch and kneads my stomach – first one paw up, then the other. When I was working on this painting, it struck me that the raised paw was the right attitude for my gigantic magic cat.

The figure in *Dr Dimension* (see page 43), floats upside-down in space. I get a kick out of the fact that people often want to reverse the painting so the doctor is upright. Can't have all that blood rushing to his head! I remind them that in space, there is no right way up.

Alien Basketball (see page 42) features the scene for which all mankind waits: not only are we not alone in the universe, but the aliens are good basketball players! I made the aliens short and squat to get maximum contrast against the tall, stringy human players.

Majyk by Accident
(Ace Books, 1992)

Alien Basketball *(Idle Pleasures)*
(Berkley Books, 1982)

HARDWARE

Spaceships offer a fascinating challenge to a science fiction artist, primarily because vehicles capable of exploring distant galaxies reside exclusively in the realm of the imagination. A futuristic intergalactic vehicle or space station is completely open to interpretation. Unlike the human body, which, in spite of wide variations in colour, size and shape, has a set appearance that even a child knows, a spaceship allows much more freedom to explore an aesthetic solution unhindered by preconceived ideas. Different artists have different visions of what tomorrow's spacecraft will look like – from Chris Foss's asymmetrical behemoths, to Vincent DiFate's streamlined space needles, to Robert McCall's gravity defying floating cities. But they all have one thing in common; an authority and power that makes the viewer believe they exist.

I have tried a lot of different approaches to designing space ships, and I haven't settled on a standard solution. The painting on this page for *The Mind Pool* features a huge vessel with lots of windows, always a good way to show scale. I also made the various sections irregular, with bulbous shapes sticking out between uneven constructs. Though I can appreciate the beauty of a ship as smooth and uncluttered as a 747 jumbo jet, I tend to think that if city-sized crafts like this one are ever constructed, they will probably not be symmetrical and streamlined, but will grow like a well-planned contemporary city – on a grand design, but with lots of overall variation.

The story in *The Mind Pool* involves a ship that mines the asteroids, and in order to increase the overall complexity of the scene, I included lots of little ships scurrying around bringing raw material into the main ship's smelter. The colour solution in this piece employs yellow and violet, complementary colours that I find particularly striking. Andrew Loomis, in his book *Creative Illustration* (which I recommend to aspiring illustrators), said that a painting keyed to one colour, and accented with its colour complement, will never fall flat. I often draw on that advice when I am struggling to come up with a good colour solution.

While working on this painting, my beloved cat Orson died, and I put in a tribute to her in the asteroid field. Those of you with sharp eyes may be able to spot it. Orson, named after Orson Welles, was a female Manx who, like her namesake, had a weight problem in later life. She was my constant companion in the studio for many years, sitting next to me and watching me paint.

The Anarch Lords
(DAW Books, 1981)

Life Probe
(Del Rey Books, 1982)

Light City was painted at Walt Disney Studios. As is the case with *Flying High* (see pages 56–7), I was encouraged to practice matte painting skills between films. Since most of the practice exercises were landscapes, I would often add strange elements to turn the painting into a science fiction composition.

Many people are surprised when they see a finished matte. Because mattes are combined with live action footage, they expect a scene of photographic realism, with every detail tickled to death. After all, the matte must look believable enough to fool the movie audience. But in truth, these paintings, which are usually done on glass, are much looser in execution. The best description is impressionistic. The matte artist doesn't have to paint every leaf on a tree or every blade of grass to create a convincing setting. The key trick is to match the lighting and colour of the original photographic plate. A good matte painting, like a good impressionist landscape painting, lays down all the tones in the right place, as the eye is accustomed to seeing them in nature. The eye, recognizing familiar shapes and colours, obligingly fills in the details. Surprisingly, if a matte artist actually goes in and paints all the little details, the finished painting will often look less convincing because you have added more than the eye would see, and the painting will look artificial.

The cover for *Life Probe* features geodesic domes on each end of the space ship. Thinking back on this project, I realize what an enormous time saver a computer would have been, but this painting was done long before I went digital. To achieve the effect, I had to laboriously plot out all of the strut placements over a sphere, and then paint them in with a ruling pen. It took several days. With a computer, I now can generate that same dome in a three dimensional program in about an hour. To see how I handled a geodesic dome on the computer, take a look at *Years Of The City* (see page 85).

Zoboa (see pages 48–9), is for the book by Martin Caidin, author of the *Six Million Dollar Man,* about a terrorist plot to blow up the space shuttle. Ironically, I was actually sitting at my drawing board working on this painting when news came of the 1986 space shuttle disaster. That coincidence has forever linked this painting with that tragic event. Caidin's book, in contrast to reality, has a positive conclusion. The plot to destroy the shuttle is foiled by some vintage aircraft buffs, which explains the World War II fighter plane in the foreground.

Light City *(Stellar 7)*
(Del Rey Books, 1980)

Star Trek: Log 4
(Del Rey Books, 1992)

Star Trek: Log 7
(Del Rey Books, 1992)

Doing the ten covers for the Alan Dean Foster Star Trek: Log books was an entertaining challenge because I was contractually prohibited from using the likenesses of the characters from the original 1960s television show. Moreover, I could use only the spacecraft from that show, not from any of the subsequent movies. The design of the Enterprise from that original series, while certainly innovative for its day, looks dated by contemporary standards. Ever since the Star

Wars movies set a new level of excellence, movie makers have used models with copious detail to imply scale and complexity. By the time the first Star Trek movie was made, the Enterprise had been completely remodelled with new surface patterning to dazzle the eye, but I couldn't use that ship; I had to use the original, rather smooth Enterprise. Rather than add detail to the ship which would be inaccurate, I opted to reduce the size of the Enterprise in the paintings,

Star Trek: Log 6
(Del Rey Books, 1992)

Star Trek: Log 10
(Del Rey Books, 1992)

featuring it only as part of a larger scene with lots of other interesting elements in it.

Even though Alan Dean Foster based these books on the animated TV series, he took the half-hour TV scripts, reworked them, and produced fully realized novels. Following Foster's lead, I expanded on the scenes, using some elements that were only implied. I felt free to elaborate on his ideas to create more interesting compositions.

The rough layout for the cover for *Star Trek:*

Log 6 was done by my friend, Paul Chadwick, who was my roommate at Art Center College of Design, and is the creator of the award-winning comic book *Concrete*, published by Dark Horse Comics. Paul has an unusual way of patterning a composition with a distinctive interweaving of curving and straight lines. I was delighted with the thumbnail sketch he gave me of this space dock, and acknowledged his help by putting his initials on the superstructure.

Berserker
(Amazing Stories, 1980)

I got a good grounding in perspective at Art Center College of Design, which is essential in doing hardware paintings. To create a convincing space ship, you need to know where an object's vanishing point is, how to project a shadow across a plane, and when to bend the rules for effect. *Berserker* has an unusual perspective solution using two sets of vanishing points: a tight set for the foreground ships, and a wide angle set on the Berserker in the background to enlarge its appearance. While violating the rules of perspective, it does imitate how the eye works.

Basing a painting on a geometric shape is a powerful compositional technique. *Space Station Five* (see page 55), is a study in circles, and I iterated the circular theme throughout the composition. The three large portals anchor the piece, and the circular motif is repeated in the planet to the rear, the helmet in the foreground, the docking space ship, the machinery on the back wall and black balls hanging from the ceiling.

I experimented with casein colours while painting in *The Phantom Spaceship* (see page 55). Caseins were popular before the advent of acrylics. They have some of the properties of gouache in that they can be blended, and some of oil, notably their slower drying time.

Killer Station
(Baen Books, 1985)

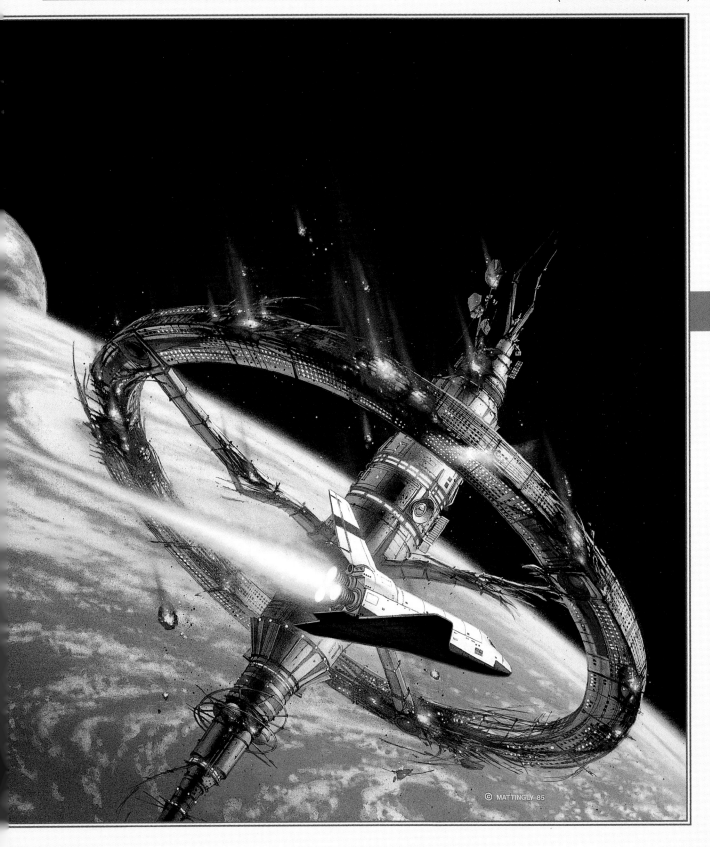

© MATTINGLY 85

The Armageddon Inheritance
(Baen Books, 1993)

The Phantom Space Ship (Goldstar)
(Signet Books, 1989)

The Wolf Worlds
(Del Rey Books, 1984)

I think the title for this painting, *Flying High*, with its wily *double entendre*, adds to the enjoyment of the piece. The inspiration came from James Steranko, the great artist and writer. He was one of my childhood idols, and when I met him years later at the San Diego Comic Convention, we became friends. He visited me at Disney Studios and saw this piece which I was doing for practice. With many film projects going on, it took a long time for me to finish. Steranko kept abreast of the progress and asked if he could be the first to print it in his magazine, *Prevue*. Before it went to press, he called to ask for its title, and learning I hadn't come up with anything, he suggested *Flying High*, because the rider looks so deliriously happy.

Early in my career, I experimented extensively with painting in different mediums, and mixing mediums. This piece is acrylic over a watercolour underpainting, an unusual mixture. For the last ten years I have settled down to doing my finals entirely in acrylic for reasons of permanence. Mixing several mediums can give unpredictable results over time, and since I sell a lot of my paintings I don't want to hear that one of my works has faded or the paint is flaking up from the canvas.

After *Flying High* was published in *Prevue*, it was picked up by a poster company, Metamorphosis Graphics, where it sold successfully through mail order and poster outlets. Like most science fiction artists, I retain the rights to almost all of my work so I can resell the reproduction rights to a piece after it has been published by the company that originally commissioned it. I have resold the rights to *Flying High* numerous times, but the most interesting had to be the sale to Roger Corman's New World Pictures.

It started when I interviewed with Corman's wife Julie, a successful producer in her own right, about designing a movie based on Isaac Asimov's *Nightfall,* a classic science fiction story. I opted not to get involved, but I gave Julie Corman a poster of *Flying High* as a sample, which she hung on her wall. While conferring with his wife, Roger saw it and thought it would be an interesting starting point for a movie. Before long, lawyers from New World Pictures contacted me, and after some spectacularly convoluted negotiations, they bought the movie rights to the painting. Corman commissioned several screenplays for the project, reportedly based on a 'Hell's Angels in the Sky' concept, but nothing has ever come of it. It's too bad, because it's funny to think how the writing credit would have read – 'Screenplay by John Doe, based on a painting by...'.

Now that's one you don't see every day.

Software

I find the human figure the most difficult and challenging of subjects, and usually the most rewarding. The painting to the right, *Orion*, is my favourite of the 500 or so paintings that span my career. I did it several months after moving to New York, and it is a personal statement on what it means to me to be an artist. The painting features a mythic god, symbol of the heart, who sits enthroned over the prostrate figure of a space man, symbol of technology. I see good art that way – as the triumph of the soul over the machine.

Don't get me wrong, in recent years, I have gotten increasingly more involved with computer graphics. I love what advanced technology can do for an artist, from 3-D modeling to the freedom to try out different colour schemes and textures with the click of a mouse. But what makes art so meaningful is not contained in any of the tools at an artist's disposal, but rather what he or she has to say. Art, above all, is a nonverbal dialogue between the artist and viewer.

When I sit at the drawing board painting with a brush, I have a direct connection with the prehistoric artists who daubed mud on the walls of caves with a stick. The tools are fancier now, and thanks to centuries of innovation, we understand perspective, colour theory, and foreshortening, but the urge that compelled a Neanderthal man to draw the beasts he hunted on a cave wall is the same that quickens the pulse of a contemporary artist sitting before a computer. It is the need to say something, to communicate with others through pictures. Whether it is the cave paintings at Lascaux, the Sistine Chapel or Picasso's *Guernica*, the art that moves me has a revelatory quality, sounding a resonant chord in my being.

Orion uses some of the compositional techniques that Jacques Louis David and the Neoclassical painters utilized so effectively. David was a master of controlling the movement of the eye in a painting, and I used some of his ideas in *Orion*. For instance, there are curving eye traps on each corner of the painting to redirect your eye back to the central figure of the god. In the lower right hand corner is the arcing cloud mass; in the upper right, the curve of the pinwheel nebula; in the upper left, jet trails pointing back to the god; and on the lower left, the shifting tonal mass and pillar. In theory, your eye should travel in this curving pattern through the painting, hitting the eye traps and going back to the god and astronaut. I also used a "Z" shape as a unifying design link. The recumbent space man is in a "Z" pattern that is echoed in the flame, which is echoed in the folds of the god's drape and in the cloud mass to his left.

Angel's Luck: Precious Cargo
(Del Rey Books, 1989)

Angel's Luck: Desperate Measures, Precious Cargo and *The Essence of Evil* are a trilogy by Joe Clifford Faust, one of my favourite science fiction writers. All of these paintings are in the 'storytelling' tradition of many comic book covers. From the cover's strong visual narrative, you can speculate on what happened just before, and what will happen next. I love this sort of solution because, without giving the plot away, it conveys a moment of suspended action. I wish I saw more of this on book covers rather than the static setup of a heroic figure posing in the foreground.

I also used a comic book technique for Faust's *Company Man* (see page 62), which is broken up into five panelled sections. In the first panel on the left, the man senses no danger, but as the narrative progresses to the right, he sees the attacking air car and breaks into a run, growing larger as he moves into the foreground.

At the art director's suggestion, I used myself as the model for Faust's first two books, *A Death of Honor* and *Company Man* (see page 62). In *Company Man*, the protagonist is down on his luck, so I tried to make myself look as disreputable and shady as possible. Ironically, this happens to be my mother's favourite of my self-portraits. I gave her the original as a Christmas present, and it hangs in her house were she points it out to visitors saying 'That's my son!' It's really true, beauty is in the eye of the beholder.

When I was assigned the *Angel's Luck* trilogy, I was asked specifically not to use myself as the central figure. It was crushing news, and I feared my days of big-time modelling were over. However, I made a sneak appearance, casting myself, and my wife Cathleen as the dominatrix, in the green hologram. The drunk, cheek mashed into the table, is a portrait of author Joe Clifford Faust, done with his chuckling consent.

One of my favourite models, Dennis Vestunis, posed as the wrench-wielding tough in *Angel's Luck: Precious Cargo*. With Dennis, a bodybuilder, you don't have to exaggerate his physique. He also posed for the central figure in *Orion* (see pages 58–9). Dennis is balding, and this downward three-point perspective was the perfect angle for displaying that attribute.

The *Angel's Luck* scene features an organic engine transmission for a space ship. Contrasts in paintings always add visual impact, and this offered a nice opportunity to contrast this pink, living globular mass, resembling an overgrown multiple heart encased in a force field, against the cold, reflective steel of the control room. To make the contrast even more dramatic, I made the organic transmission all warm colours, while the metal surfaces are all in cool colours.

Angel's Luck: The Essence of Evil
(Del Rey Books, 1989)

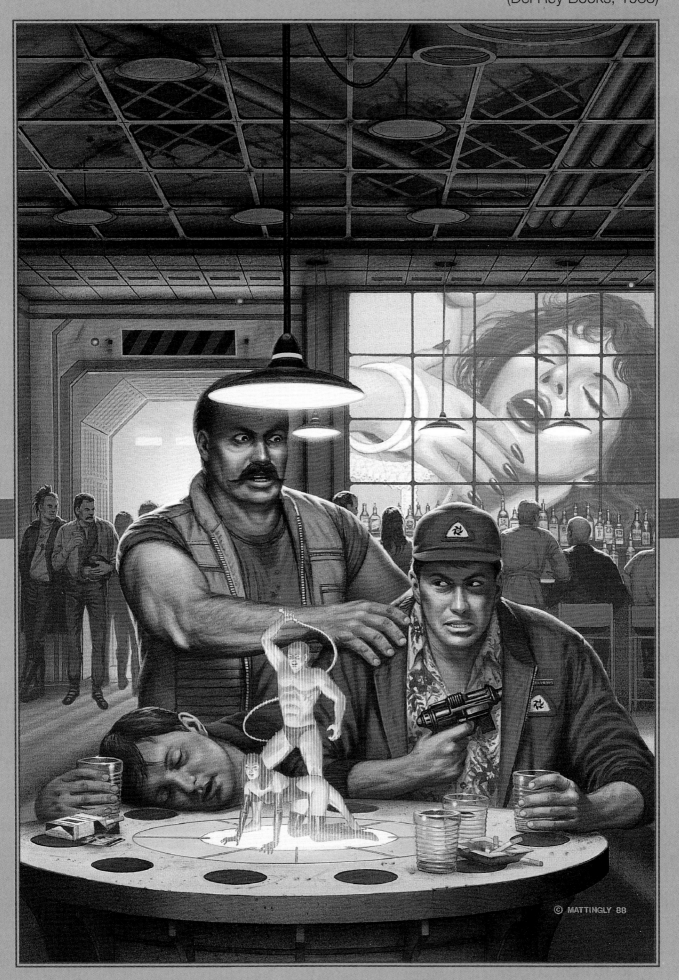

Company Man
(Del Rey Books Books, 1987)

A Death of Honor
(Del Rey Books Books, 1986)

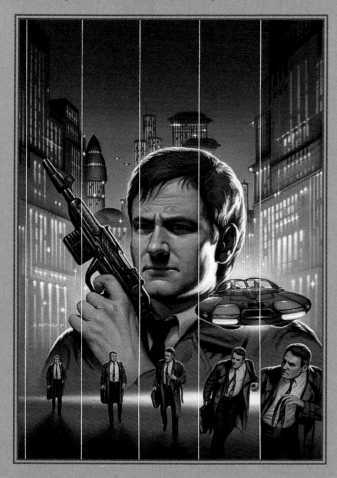

After reading the manuscript for *A Death of Honor*, I did something I had never done before – I wrote first-time author Joe Clifford Faust a fan letter. He responded, and we struck up a friendship. Although his books typically involve dissolute characters and wild sexual situations, it turns out that Joe is a devoted family man and a born-again Christian. From reading his work, one would expect a completely different personality, but I guess like all terrific writers, Joe has a rich imagination. Faust writes character-driven science fiction, a refreshing departure from the predominantly plot-driven books in this genre.

The Voice of Cepheus is a cover that harkens back to an art game I devised as a kid. I would find two photographs with similar head sizes, say one of Liza Minnelli and another of King Kong, and cut both into horizontal strips. Then I would reassemble the two in alternating strips, ending up with a composite that was half Liza Minnelli, half King Kong. The results were extremely funny to an 8-year-old, and between that and blowing bubbles into milk through a straw inserted in my nose, a great way to attract girls. However, before this project, I was never able to put this merging of likenesses to use.

The plot of *The Voice of Cepheus* revolves around the earth receiving transmissions from a distant alien civilization. The communication instructs human scientists to construct a virtual reality helmet that sets up an instant communications link that simulates face-to-face contact. In this hi-tech world, computers play a key role in deciphering the first alien communique, so I wanted to incorporate scan lines into the design. While experimenting with this pattern, I remembered my childhood 'trick photography' technique. I inter-spliced two images, one of a man in a virtual reality helmet, and the other of a distant nebula. Combined, they resemble computer screen scan lines, a great metaphor for the book.

Painting the final was tedious. First I painted the helmeted figure to a finished quality, and then masked off all the areas I wanted to keep with thin strips of masking tape, and sealed the whole with acrylic medium. Next, I painted the nebula and stars over the masking tape and exposed surface. After it dried, I painstakingly peeled off the masking tape, and retouched the areas where bleeding had inevitably occurred.

Manually superimposing one image on top of the other took longer than doing a straight painting, but the extra effort paid off. It's tempting to stick to tried-and-true styles, never deviating from what one has done successfully in the past. It is hard to come up with new ideas, and doing something different leaves you open to failure. I do my share of repeating myself, but I always try to arrive at a unique solution. The covers I am most proud of are those where I attempted something unusual.

© MATTINGLY 89

Space Lady
(Starlog, 1983)

I finished *Space Lady* by staying up for several nights in a row to meet the deadline. It was done fifteen years ago, when I used to do that a lot. I have gotten older now, and I try to keep 'all-nighters' to a minimum. I take on enough work now to keep me busy, but not enough to drive me crazy.

That doesn't mean I don't work late. Even as a child, I was a night owl. I remember when I was young, my mother would put me to bed at 9 p.m., and I would read by flashlight under the covers for several hours before I grew sleepy. My most productive work hours are at night when the house is quiet and everyone else has gone to bed. There are no interrupting phone calls or delivery men at the door. I generally work until 2 a.m., and get up between 9 and 9.30 a.m. At several points in my life, I have tried to get on a more normal schedule, but apparently, my biological clock is calibrated to a nocturnal setting.

I take one hour off each day to exercise. Painting is a sedentary profession, and I believe it is very important to include exercise in one's daily routine. I split my workout between running outdoors and using the exercise bike in my studio. I read for the hour I am on the exercise bike. It provides a nice break, and I try to read for pleasure, but I must admit, I often park it in front of my computer so I can study a new piece of software.

Often the best solutions for a cover occur when I am relaxed and not fixating on the project. After spending the day working on sketches, I'll get in bed and close my eyes. Suddenly, a new idea will pop into my head, fully formed. This happens so frequently that I keep a pad and pencil beside the bed.

The Reality Matrix
(Baen Books, 1986)

Cenotaph Road: Iron Tongue
(Avon Books, 1984)

Cenotaph Road: Fire and Fog
(Avon Books, 1984)

I had a six-inch model spider built out of wire and moulded foam for the *Cenotaph Road* series. Before the model was made, I had difficulty getting the perspective right on the six legs, especially when the spider was at an odd angle. The great thing about pliable models is that you can set up the pose and light it.

When I submitted the sketches for *Rescued from Paradise* to publisher Jim Baen, he thought the painting would be better without the three figures at the bottom, so that the focus would be on the main figure meeting the space travellers. I felt strongly that the lower figures, especially the woman, helped highlight the joyousness of the meeting of the two cultures. After some discussion, I told him that if he still objected to the placement of additional people in the final piece, I would paint them out. Luckily, when I turned in the finish, Jim liked what he saw and I didn't have to change it.

Doc Sidhe (see page 68), is a tribute to James Bama's *Doc Savage* covers. This book takes place in an alternate universe where all the architecture is Art Deco retro, so I got the chance to do variations on some of my favourite buildings in New York. Note, for example, the left hand structure, which is inspired by the Chrysler building. I went out one evening at dusk, just as the building lights were coming on, to shoot reference. Twilight is when I find New York the most beautiful.

The first *Doc Sidhe* sketch I showed Jim Baen

used very restrained colour, à la Bama, but he asked that I replace the white shirt on the main figure with a bright red one. I think that suggestion is what makes this cover work. The red shirt acts as a focal point, set off by the subdued warm and cool tones elsewhere in the painting.

I tend to be critical of my own work. Usually when I look at a painting, what I see are the unsolved problems. *Shapers* (see page 69), is a rare exception. I like the whole composition. It has an uncluttered design and colour scheme, which proves that sometimes the simplest solutions are the most effective.

Almost all of the background was painted freehand with a Paasche AB airbrush. It is the finest airbrush available, with a unique turbine system. However, I have to add a caveat: it is difficult to learn, and prone to spit at the most inopportune times. Late one night as I was putting the finishing touches on a painting due the next morning, my airbrush spewed a big glob of paint on a delicate area. For the sake of decency, I will not print what I said at that moment, but this story illustrates a sidelight about being a professional illustrator. A deadline is a deadline, and if you want to continue to work in the field, you have to be reliable. I stayed up the rest of the night to rework the area, and delivered the painting on time. As I was handing it over, the art director, in all innocence, said: 'Nice airbrush work'.

Rescued From Paradise
(Baen Books, 1989)

WIZARDS

Close your eyes and imagine a wizard. Let me guess: an old guy in a robe with a flowing beard. Right? Could be Santa Claus in the off-season. It is an enduring image, and I have certainly done my share of robed, old sages. I suppose our notions of fantasy are still rooted in Arthurian legend, and Merlin remains our pre-eminent model, just as jousting knights on fantasy covers wear armour from that period and the stone turretted castles in the background are lifted from the English landscape.

But in today's fantasy fiction genre, magic is no longer the exclusive domain of grizzled, old men. Take, for example, my buxom sorceress in *The Wizard of the Rue Morgue,* or the spell casting gypsy from *Mulengro.* Also consider the young street tough who is inhabited by the soul of Merlin in *The Wizard of Sunset Strip,* or the harp-playing magician in *Moonheart.* And if you still doubt whether wizards have distinct personalities, take a look at the motley crew on the dais in *The Wizard Convention.*

The Black Throne is the cover for a book about an alternate universe where the stories of Edgar Allan Poe come to life. I hadn't read Poe since childhood, so I used this book as an excuse to go back and re-read the author's entire canon. I was pleasantly surprised to discover that in this age of ultra-violent horror fiction, Poe's work, which relies on the reader's imagination instead of going into graphic details, still holds up.

On the cover, I used familiar images from his stories to create a hallucinogenic montage on the back wall. Poe fans will recognize the orangutan from *The Murders in the Rue Morgue,* the old mariner from *The Descent in the Maelstrom,* the raven from a poem of Poe's (the title of which momentarily slips my mind), the decomposing corpse from *Facts in the Case of M. Valdemar,* and the three lead characters from *The Black Throne.* Interspersed with Poe's creations are ghouls, monsters and threatening shapes. The entire background was rendered freehand with a Paasche AB airbrush, utilizing the stuttering effect that can only be achieved with that tool.

The scene is presided over by a dark-robed evil wizard with glowing red eyes (no mistaking him for St. Nick!). Believe it or not, my wife Cathleen posed for this wicked-looking figure. She sometimes complains that I don't do flattering portraits of her, and I have to admit, in this case, she's right. When it is late at night and I need a model to finish a project, she gets the assignment by default.

© DAVID B. MATTINGLY 1990

The trio of paintings displayed on this spread – The *Wizard of 4th Street, The Wizard of Sunset Strip* and *The Wizard of the Rue Morgue* – are part of a series by Simon Hawke. I have been lucky enough to do sixteen of Simon's covers, and speaking from experience, he is an artist's writer. With some writers, you never get more than a sketchy idea of what the locale and characters look like. Simon, on the other hand, provides such rich visual descriptions that the worlds he creates come alive in your mind with great vibrancy.

All the skies in the paintings for this series were done freehand with an airbrush. To mask off areas when airbrushing, I rarely use the commercial product with an adhesive surface, known as frisket. I prefer to cut shapes out of acetate or scraps of paper lying around the studio, and loosely tape them to the painting. This method allows me to move the mask around while spraying, and avoid the hard edges endemic to airbrushes.

The proliferation of signs in the background of *The Wizard of Sunset Strip* provided lots of chances to slip inside jokes in the painting. I'll share a few. The 'Puckey' at the top of the Capitol Records building refers to the art director on the project, Don Puckey. 'Hi Nick,' written on the punk's tee shirt, is a message to the author of the *Wizard* books, Simon Hawke, who was Nickolas Yermakov in another life. Lastly, there is a hot dog

advertisement with a big 'RADIC' on it, a reference to my high school comic strip, *Radic the Destroyer*. To those who find this self-indulgent, I say in my own defence that the signs have to say something, so why not entertain myself?

The model for the big wizard's head in the background of *Wizard World* is my father, John W. Mattingly, to whom this book is dedicated. Dad is an engineer and scientist, with an unquenchable curiosity. All of his life, he has sought new ways to look at the world. He is best known for having invented the Water Pik oral hygiene appliance, for which he holds the sole patent.

Sometimes you can't gauge a parent's influence until you are an adult. Dad was a great creative role model who taught me the importance of perseverance and pushing the envelope simply to see what will happen. How else will you know?

I never put Dad in a painting before this one, partly because we live in different parts of the country, and partly because I took for granted that I would at a future date. But then, in the mid 1980s, Dad had a stroke, and suddenly it became very important to feature him in a painting. I flew to Colorado and had him pose right in his hospital bed. Looking back on it now, I know this was my way of expressing how important he is to me. Although Dad has nearly made a full recovery, this is still an emotional painting for me.

The Wizard of Sunset Strip
(Questar Books, 1988)

The Wizard of the Rue Morgue
(Questar Books, 1990)

Many illustrators only use beautiful model types, but whenever possible I like to draw on the entire spectrum of physical types – heavy people, skinny people, bald people, different ethnic groups – in short, people who don't look like fashion models. For examples of some of my non-standard models, I refer you to *Aquila and the Sphinx* (see page 32), *The Aquiliad* (see page 33), *The Regiment* (see page 101), and *The Subway Wizard* (see page 125).

In *The Wizard Convention*, I balked against using the clichéd Merlin look, and instead featured four distinctive personalities on the dais. In this case, the book company thought I had gone too far and made the characters 'ugly'. The art director insisted I rework the painting to make the wizards more 'normal'. Frankly, the art director was justified in demanding the changes. The sketch he approved featured more conventional wizards. I became inspired to give the foursome more character while painting the piece. Creative licence only goes so far when you are a commercial illustrator hired to do a cover. Once a sketch is approved, you should paint it faithfully. I learned my lesson from this experience and no longer pull switches mid-way through a project. However, in this case, I liked the version reproduced here so much that rather than paint over it and remove the idiosyncratic details, I did an entirely new painting. The painting that appeared on the cover of *The Goblin Tower* differs substantially from this.

As a rule, artists who work from their head rather than from reference tend to paint people who bear a strong resemblance to themselves. For instance, I am 6ft 5in tall and slender in build. Publisher Jim Baen sometimes complains that my figure work is modelled after me – which is especially true in my sketches. After Jim has decided on which sketch to take to final, he often reminds me to use a well-built, muscular man for the central figure, and not fall back on my own body type. I agree with him. I am a strong advocate of the need to shoot good reference. Made-up figures tend to point up the idiosyncrasies in an artist's style, such as large heads, or oddly proportioned bodies.

The Burning Realm (see pages 78–9), features a model I use a lot, Tyler K. Smith, a talented artist and sculptor in his own right. Tyler has a large, muscular build that fits the heroic mould, and a mobile face that can project any emotion I need.

With professional models, I occasionally run into the situation where eliciting an expression is like pulling teeth. Most career models make their living doing fashion or runway work, and they are accustomed to looking glamorous, not making faces or assuming difficult poses. When I get a model who is stiff or self-conscious, I follow Norman Rockwell's advice. I stand right next to them and assume the pose and expression I want. When they see I'm not afraid to look silly, they often loosen up.

The Wizard Convention
(Del Rey Books, 1983)

Mulengro
(Ace Books, 1985)

Moonheart
(Ace Books, 1984)

DIGITAL REALMS

After twenty years of doing paintings in traditional media like acrylic and gouache, I bought an Apple Macintosh computer in 1993, and it has completely revolutionized how I work. Doing art on the computer has opened up many new possibilities, and I expect a large portion of my paintings to be computer generated in the years to come.

Computers are changing how an artist works as profoundly as the advent of photography. The camera, for better or worse, meant the artist no longer had to rely on live models, or traipse into the field to sketch reference. Now even a non-artist can take a picture of a person or place, and share that picture with a potentially unlimited audience. With photography, picture-making was no longer the exclusive domain of the artist, and artists could have access to an unlimited library of reference.

The computer is having a similarly momentous impact. The computer gives an artist a whole new set of tools that encourage experimentation without having to rework the original. In this error-tolerant medium, objects can be moved, rotated in space, textured, distorted, resized, mapped with different colour schemes – and no choice is permanent until the artist presses the save button.

The cover for *How to Save the World* featured on this page was modelled entirely in polygons, combining the best qualities of several different three-dimensional software programs. Once the objects were electronically built, the surfaces were "mapped" with my paintings; every 3-D building front, mountain and bridge has a small painting that is wrapped around all sides. This painting stretched what can be done on an Apple Mac system to the absolute limit. In my modelling fervour, I used 750,000 polygons for the buildings, and in the huge bump map in the water that provides natural reflections of the surrounding city, mountains and sky. Once I had the city built, I found a small glitch in my master plan; my computer was not powerful enough to raytrace the image at the high resolution I needed. I placed an SOS on the Internet, a great way to connect with those in the technological know. I was able to lease time on a Silicon Graphics workstation on the West Coast that rendered the painting in 225 hours. Much as I would love to animate this scene, giving the viewer a fly-through across the terrain, computer speed will have to get a lot faster before I can 'go Hollywood'.

Years of the City and *The Best of Trek* were created in three-dimensional software programs. I strongly believe this is the area of computer graphics that will show the most growth over the next decade. A few years from now, it will be possible to do a fantasy illustration on the computer by selecting elements from huge digital reference libraries. You will be able to choose a face and body type from one database, and clothe the figure from another devoted to costumes. You will create a landscape of your own, but let modelling programs work out water reflections and light disbursements. Add 100 attacking skeleton monsters, all replicated from one original design and manipulated into different poses, hit the 'render' button, and in a short time, the painting will be professionally rendered and ready to download to the publisher.

When people ask me which is the best 3-D program on the market, I explain there is no perfect solution yet. Software is improving every day, and hardware keeps getting faster, so things may be appreciably different by the time this book appears. I will mention a few of the 3D programs I have tried, but anyone interested in this area should seek the most current information.

I have used just about every 3-D program available on the Apple Macintosh, and each has its strengths. There are two parts to a 3-D program: the modeller and the renderer. The modeller is where you sculpt objects, but instead of using clay, you use polygons. The renderer is where you texture, light and photograph the models you have sculpted.

When I first got involved in this area, I cut my teeth on Ray Dream Designer, a modestly-priced entry-level program. It is good for learning the basics, but the program can only handle still images, and is not very flexible. I then moved on to a combination of Infini-D and Strata Studio Pro. Infini-D is a good all-round program, with nice anti-aliasing (the ability to smooth adjoining pixels of colour which otherwise would have jagged edges), but its modeller is middling. Strata Studio Pro, with a better modeller, turns buggy when you get involved with very large models, and is slow doing anti-aliasing. I'm now using Form-Z, which is far and away the best modeller available on the Apple Macintosh. Form-Z recently added a renderer, and is a terrific package for still images.

I recently acquired the most expensive and powerful rendering program available for the Apple Macintosh, called Electric Image. Owing to its complexity, getting up the speed entails a sizable commitment of time. There are literally scores of variables that need to be adjusted for every action, but these variables are precisely what make it so powerful. Costing the same as a small car, it is not a tool for the beginner. But once you are in the loop, the program is blazingly fast and a dream in terms of flexibility and options. It renders both stills and animation.

© MATTINGLY 94

Years of the City
(Baen Books, 1994)

Star Wars: The New Hope
(Random House, 1994)

Star Wars: The Empire Strikes Back
(Random House, 1994)
Courtesy of Lucasfilm Ltd.

These two *Star Wars* covers were assembled on the Apple Macintosh computer using two programs, Painter and Photoshop. Working in the computer environment allowed me to scan in painted elements and move them around until I liked the composition. I used Photoshop's special effects filters on the backgrounds, as well as on some of the blends. When the composition was 90 per cent finished, I got a 14 x 22 in IRIS print on watercolour paper. An IRIS print is one of the finest outputs generated from a digital file. They can be very large, up to 33 x 46 in, and printed on any material flexible enough to wrap around the device's drum. Colour calibration is always a problem on the computer, but once your monitor is calibrated to the IRIS printer, the colours are very true.

As I mentioned before, the computer offers many effects that are impossible to paint, but it is still incapable of the colour and tone nuances easily achieved with a brush. Working with an IRIS print allows me to have the best of both worlds. With these Star Wars covers, I mounted the print on illustration board, and then painted over sections with acrylic. IRIS prints, however, are water soluble, and can run just like a watercolour. To eliminate this problem, I always fix the print-out with acrylic medium before I begin painting.

Mindstar Rising is an all digital painting done in Photoshop to take advantage of the program's transparent colour layering and lettering capabilities. The central head was painted traditionally. I then had a high quality scan of it made to preserve the skin tones. Unlike the Star Wars covers, I did not use an IRIS print to paint over, but instead had a transparency made of the digital file to preserve the delicate overlays of colour. The transparency is the finished product that I handed in to the client.

Mindstar Rising
(Tor Books, 1995)

While the bulk of my work is in cover illustration, I do accept advertising jobs now and then. Typically, advertising pays more than cover work, but it is also far more restrictive. When I do a cover, I am given a manuscript to read, and in most cases, allowed to come up with my own ideas. In contrast, advertising usually involves illustrating someone else's idea, and often comes with a tight layout. This certainly simplifies the artist's task, but it tends to be creatively unsatisfying. In the truest sense of the word, advertising is work for hire. And although I experience professional pride when an assignment turns out well, I rarely have an emotional attachment to the piece.

There are exceptions, of course. One of my more interesting jobs was a series of matte paintings depicting the growth of the Chicago skyline from pioneer times to present day. I did my own research, and was able to pick the images to evoke the different time periods. The paintings were combined in a sixty-second TV spot for a bank that showed Chicago sprouting up on the banks of Lake Michigan in fast-time.

Having that amount of creative autonomy is rare. One of the reasons working in advertising is such a chore is that so many people have their fingers in the pie. Owing to the hefty budgets, client jobs require the approval of a battery of people, ranging from the art director, to the department head, to the immediate client contact, to the contact's boss, and on up the corporate ladder. Naturally, each person is given creative input, requiring the illustrator to make changes. Advertising jobs are notorious among artists for an endless stream of corrections and revisions. It can be frustrating too, as often the requested changes are based on political rather than aesthetic considerations. This is why I do a lot of my advertising jobs digitally – it is almost always easier to make changes on the computer than the canvas.

When I do a book cover, I normally deal only with the art director. Even in large publishing houses, the approval process is limited to the art director and book editor. I don't enjoy making changes to a completed painting as a rule, but I never refuse. I am an illustrator, not a fine artist, and ultimately the client has the final say. I never quibble over small alterations, and in fact, often take my palette with me when I deliver a cover for quick touch-ups. However, if I have delivered a cover that is faithful to the approved sketch, and the client asks for a substantial change, I will request an additional fee. If the changes result from a difference of interpretation over what was agreed to, or if they will significantly improve the painting, I will do them at no charge to the client.

Vampire by Night (*Tomorrow Sucks*)
(Baen Books, 1994)

Deep Space Dreamscape
(Worlds of Wonder, 1994)

I believe the next generation of artists will be completely at home in the digital environment. They will have grown up with computers, and judging by the exponential advances in technology over the past decade and a half, the digital tools at their disposal will be far superior to ours. Graphic artists like myself who trained in the pre-digital age still encounter barriers to switching entirely to the computer when we attempt to apply formal painting techniques to the computer. Many of the subtle effects in painting are still hard to achieve in a digital medium, such as nuances in skin tone, glazing effects and laying in delicate passages of colour. Also the digitizing tablet, while a far better input device than the mouse, is not as sensitive to variations of pressure as it should be in order to replicate brushwork.

I suppose I am representative of the arts in transition – part formalist, part digital artist. For instance, if I need a head for a digital composition, I find it much easier to paint the head on canvas and then scan it into the computer for final manipulation. In the case of *Indistinguishable From Magic*, I painted over an IRIS print with all the space ships and robots generated in a 3-D program, and then worked the skin tones of the magician in acrylic. Young artists honing their skills in cyberspace will have a more direct, and less prejudicial attitude toward creating a work of art exclusively on the computer. Their palette will encompass the entire spectrum of media-video, animation, sound, text and images. If Leonardo

Da Vinci were born today, he would no longer leave you speculating about the meaning of the *Mona Lisa*'s smile. On CD-ROM, he would have Mona tell you directly what was on her mind, and give you a choice of different backgrounds and poses. I also believe an increasing emphasis will be placed on interactivity. In the future you will be able to change a digital painting to match your decor, or your mood. Can't you see it – 'Sylvia, couldn't we choose some happier colours for *The Scream*? I'm feeling really perky today'.

I can foresee the time when I will paint my central figures directly on the computer. The figure in *Deep Space Dreamscape* was painted using a program called Photoshop, with a digitizing tablet. In this case, her flesh is handled in a posterized fashion, so I didn't have to worry about delicate skin tones. Painting like this takes advantage of what the computer can do rather than fighting it.

As the painting programs get more sophisticated and malleable, many of the skills I have learned using natural media will become more directly transferable to the electronic media. In the long run there is no stopping progress. When you consider the quantum leap in special effects from the first *Star Wars* film to *Jurassic Park*, you must assume a similar revolution will rock the commercial and fine arts fields.

Indistinguishable From Magic
(Baen Books, 1995)

FUTURE WARRIORS

Science fiction abounds with galactic battles. While I would like to think warfare will be obsolete in the future, I see little present cause for optimism. If history is any judge, mankind will never lose its warring nature, and future generations of space travellers will conquer new planets, species and sentient machines as frequently by laser sword as through peaceful means. And while women in the United States armed forces petition for combat duty, most science fiction writers still view war as a man's job, although this too is changing with the new generation of more liberated authors. The male warrior, a celebrated icon of virility since time immemorial, appears on many of my covers. This section contains a representative sample of my various takes on the subject.

Part of the fun of doing this kind of novel is designing the accoutrements of future warfare; the space age equivalents of armour, weaponry and aircraft. Some writers, like Frederik Pohl, provide detailed descriptions of these; others, like Isaac Asimov, leave it to the reader's imagination. Some of the futuristic technologies can be extremely challenging to an artist. How, for example, do you depict a space ship with living parts, or communication based on mental telepathy? For my solutions, see *Angel's Luck: Precious Cargo* (see page 60), and *Distant Friends* (see pages 92–3).

The Messiah Stone is proof that inspiration comes from many quarters. I was assigned the cover to Martin Caidin's book shortly after I visited an exhibition of Maori art at the Metropolitan Museum of Art. The Maori come from New Zealand, and their artwork has a unique quality – while distinctly primitive, it has incredible power, and what can only be called a spiritual quality. Much of it has swirling patterns running over the surface, and the poses are often aggressive. I was struck by a huge gateway figure, a *waharoa*, with the image of a man in it. I used the gateway's stiff, menacing pose for the central male figure. The woman's kneeling posture is a sly reference to the author's archetypal woman: a brilliant triple Ph.D. physicist, who in the presence of her man, turns into an adoring sex kitten.

Due to the extremely violent and sexual content in some Caidin novels, publisher Jim Baen took the unusual editorial step of starring those sections that potentially might offend the more timid or conservative reader. Some joked the asterisks provided an easy way to skip to the 'good parts'.

Author Simon Hawke, who wrote the Time Wars books, is doing something with one of my paintings that I don't think anyone has done before; he has had it tattooed on his upper arm and shoulder. I was very flattered when he called to ask if I would have any objection to his making *Time Wars: The Ivanhoe Gambit* into a tattoo, and I quickly gave permission. It is always nice to hear that an author likes a cover I did for their book, but certainly Simon takes that to its ultimate conclusion. He is probably the first author in history to make his cover art a part of his body. I look at a tattoo as the ultimate commitment to a piece of art; once you have one, you can't get away from it. I like my own paintings a lot, but I'm not sure I would like to wear one for the rest of my life. By the way, if any other authors want to have a cover I did for their book tattooed on their body, I hereby give permission. You don't even have to call and ask.

When I am done with the sketches for a project, I will often go back and redo a scene from a high or low angle. The vast majority of book covers are done at eye level, or about five feet off the ground. Looking at the same scene from ground level, or from a height of 20 feet, can produce striking results, primarily because it isn't the normal way we view the world.

My wife and I are avid theatre-goers, but given current Broadway ticket prices, we often sit in the balcony, looking down on the actors. For large productions, I prefer this bird's-eye view of the action, and this is why I became convinced of the dramatic potential of high vantage points. High-viewing angles are a more primitive way of handling space, as evidenced by much of pre-perspective art where high angles were often used. For instance, if you look at Hieronymus Bosch's *The Last Judgement*, even though he didn't use perspective as we know it today, it is still very clear what elements are close to the viewer and what are far away. From a high angle, objects appear lower in the picture as they get closer, and higher as they get further away, as well as getting larger or smaller. From eye level, objects only get larger or smaller – they don't move vertically in the picture plane.

I think a great deal of the impact of *The Samurai Defender* cover (see pages 98-9), comes from its high angle. The viewer looks down on the confrontation, which creates a feeling of omnipotence, reinforced by seeing more of the action than the central figure can. This is a wrap-around cover, and when readers first pick up the book, they only see the Samurai warrior standing over the slain alien. But when the book is turned over, they spot the alien reinforcements sneaking up.

© MATTINGLY 83

Time Wars: The Ivanhoe Gambit
(Ace Books, 1983)

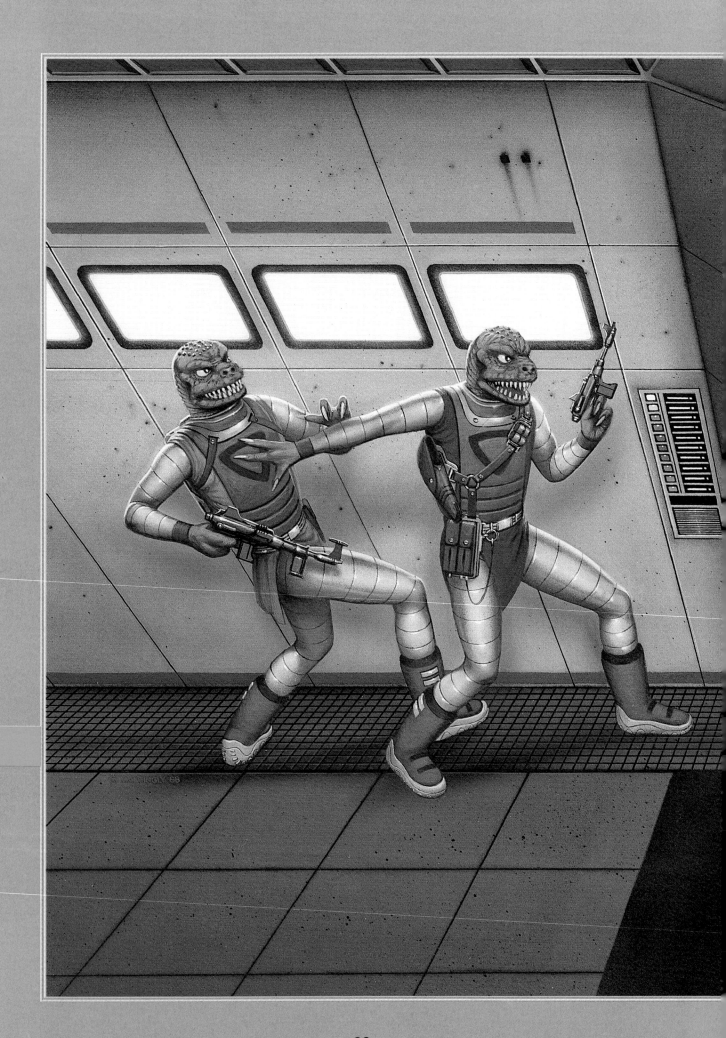

White Regiment
(Baen Books, 1983)

Comic books of the 1960s and 1970s were an important influence for me, and Joe Kubert was one of my favourite artists. He has had an unusual career as most of his best work has been in comics with World War I and II themes, rather than superhero titles. Even his *Tarzan* and *Tor* comics escape neat categorization. When I was working on sketches for the two *Regiment* books, I looked for inspiration in back issues of Kubert's war comics. The narrative content in his covers is awesome – few can set up a scene like Kubert does. For these two paintings, I wanted to capture the drama and action which are the trademarks of his art.

In *White Regiment*, I used a special effect that would have been a snap on the computer, but was very time-consuming to paint. The soldiers are travelling through a matter transfer screen, reminiscent of the transporters in *Star Trek*. Prior to emerging, I depict them as a negative image, and to reinforce the concept of matter being de-assembled and put back together in a distant place, I have a dot pattern screen running over them. Handling this manually, I first had to paint the soldiers traditionally. I then made a negative Xerox of them, which I sandwiched together with the positive painting. The negative image was the top layer, so I cut out those sections from it that I wanted to show positive. Next, I laid an acetate dot screen across the negative area only, and had a colour copy made of the whole thing. After considerable retouching, I glued the Xerox of the soldiers to a larger canvas, and painted in the rest of the scene. Although sanded, the Xerox edges are slightly raised, giving it an embossed effect.

I filled the back cover of this wrap-around for *The Regiment* with so much painting, the publisher gave up and left the printed version free of all type, except for the required UPC box.

The Regiment
(Baen Books, 1983)

Greenthieves
(Ace Books, 1994)

First Citizen is based on Rembrandt's *Socrates Contemplating the Bust of Plato*. The original is at the Metropolitan Museum of Art in New York. Like most painters, I love to study the work of the great masters. Living just outside of New York City gives me access to world-class art collections, especially in the field of modern art. And whenever I travel, for business or pleasure, I go out of my way to visit the local museums and galleries. The European capitals are prime vacation spots, but there can be art gems in unexpected places, like the outstanding collection of American art at the Gilcrease Institute in Tulsa, Oklahoma.

While good reproductions make art accessible, nothing compares to standing before an original work to understand the artist's intention, and to evaluate the technique and brushwork. These encounters can change how you view an artist. For example, Claude Monet never numbered among my favourite artists until my wife and I saw his gigantic murals of water lilies, housed in two specially built rooms in the Louvre in Paris. In both rooms, the wall-sized murals form a continuous, circular panorama, as though the viewer is standing on an island in the centre of a water lily pond. Much of the impact has to do with the textured application of paint. Close up, the colours are thick globs and swirls of pure

abstraction; only from a distance do the dappled wetlands, reflective water surfaces and skies emerge. You can't help wondering how he controlled the application of paint, done with such a loose hand, while retaining the perspective of distance. The reproductions of these murals are pretty, but not that impressive. When standing before the actual paintings, you know you are in the presence of extraordinary genius.

Each time I revisit a favourite work in a museum, I see something new. Admittedly, seeing room after room of masterpieces is humbling to an artist's ego, but exhilarating at the same time. To see a great painting is to fall in love with art all over again.

Arranging the paintings in this book led to logical couplings, and some less so. For example, what does *Greenthieves* have in common with *First Citizen*? Would you believe the jacket on both lead figures? I bought it fifteen years ago because it resembled Decker's jacket in *Bladerunner*. After wearing it until it was ragged, I consigned it to my costume closet where it has had a second life. Since I supply models with most of the clothing they wear for a shoot, favourite items of apparel get recycled over and over.

Stellar Death Plan
(Avon Books, 1988)

Lensman: First Lensman
(Berkley Books, 1982)

All three of the paintings on this spread were inspired by books from, or written in the style of, the golden age of science fiction. I enjoy going back and reading the stories from that more innocent time. It is interesting that even the most incisive prognosticators missed things that are the very building blocks of modern technology. For instance, few writers foresaw the microchip and the profound impact it has had on our lives. In fact, many portrayed characters consulting thick books of algorithms and then manually changing vacuum tubes (and we gripe about current processing speeds!). Also, who could foresee that after landing on the moon, the space program would stall out. When I first saw Kubrick's *2001* as a 10-year-old boy, I was absolutely convinced we would be going to Jupiter by 2001. We are now only six years from that milestone, but man hasn't even revisited the moon since the 1970s.

Doc Smith, the author of the classic Lensman books, got a lot of the details about the future wrong, but did so with such gusto that the books are a delight to read anyway. One of the problems I faced in repackaging the Lensman books was staying true to the narrative. For instance, as the series progressed, the size of the armoured space suits kept getting larger. By book six, Doc Smith had

everyone in suits the dimension of armoured personnel carriers. I wanted to stay at a scale where you could tell it was a human being inside, so I kept the suits form-fitting throughout the series.

The Welcoming Party (see pages 106–7), was inspired by the work of the Brandywine School of illustrators, especially Howard Pyle and N.C. Wyeth. Both of them are remarkable artists, and Wyeth's work is still widely available through the reprints of the classics he illustrated. Pyle's books have not been kept in print as much, and consequently he is harder to find and study. While many illustrators fall back on a certain cliché type that they use over and over, Pyle had the remarkable ability to instill the figures in his paintings with distinct personalities.

I visited the Delaware Museum a few years ago to see its collection of Pyle's work, and I marvelled at how in his pirate paintings every face has a distinct personality. The buccaneers are such individually created characters that you could tell a story around each of them.

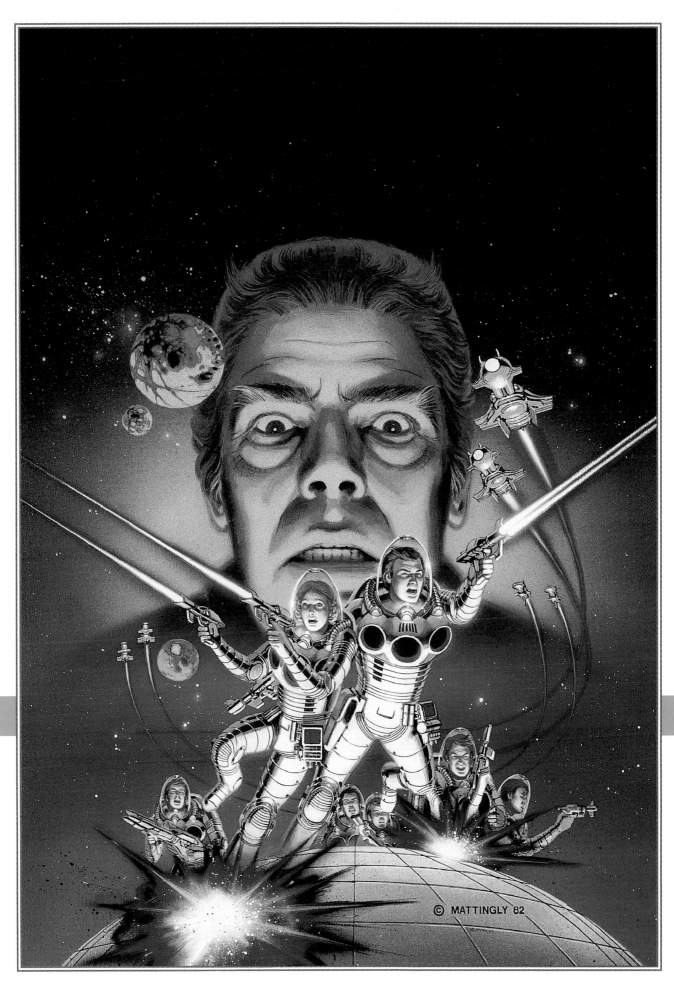

© MATTINGLY 82

Lensman: Triplanetary
(Berkley Books, 1982)

MIXED FANTASY

Mixed Fantasy is a mixed bag of fantasy subjects. While both fantasy and science fiction are products of the imagination, they are quite distinct from one another. Science fiction generally involves hardware, scientific theory and the future. Fantasy belongs to the realm of swords, sorcery and magic. Good fantasy might be described as legends and fairytales written for an adult readership. Perhaps it is easiest to define the two genres by example: the quintessential fantasy writer is J.R.R. Tolkien; his science fiction counterpart is Robert Heinlein

In the majority of cases, fantasy novels are chock-full of highly visual scenes. Often the challenge is to sift through this wealth of material to find an image that represents the whole book. My fantasy work tends to be less plot specific than my science fiction covers. Often I will try to communicate the feel and mood of the book rather than any specific narrative content. Examples of this are *Firetime* (see page 112), *Yarril's Children* (see page 118), or *American Gothic 3000* (see page 114).

I lead off this section with one of my favourites, *The Little Helliad*, the busy canvas on this page. If *Orion* is a personal statement on what it means to be a science fiction artist, *The Little Helliad* sums up my outlook on being a fantasy artist. I chose the blind poet Homer, one of history's first fantasy writers, as the central figure of this piece. He symbolizes the tradition of mythic storytelling where mortals do battle with the gods and the supernatural. I wanted Homer to be saying 'Come into my world of wonders and see sights you have never beheld before'. Surrounding Homer is a panoply of characters, spanning the worlds of the real and fantastic. Sharing the same space are contemporary soldiers, a reclining Confucius, a skeleton gondolier ferrying souls across the River Styx and various animal-headed creatures.

My wife Cathleen appears as Cleopatra in this one, with her most beloved cat, Agatha. The cat was obsessively devoted to Cathe, and on the rare occasions when Cathe and I had a row, Agatha would stand only feet away, howling at the top of her lungs. The only way to console her was to resolve the issue, or continue arguing in a happy tone of voice. Try that some time! It's impossible to work up a good head of steam while smiling and keeping your voice modulated. Cathe is on the right, peeking around the edge of the book and pointing, while Agatha, with a human body, has her arm protectively around Cathe.

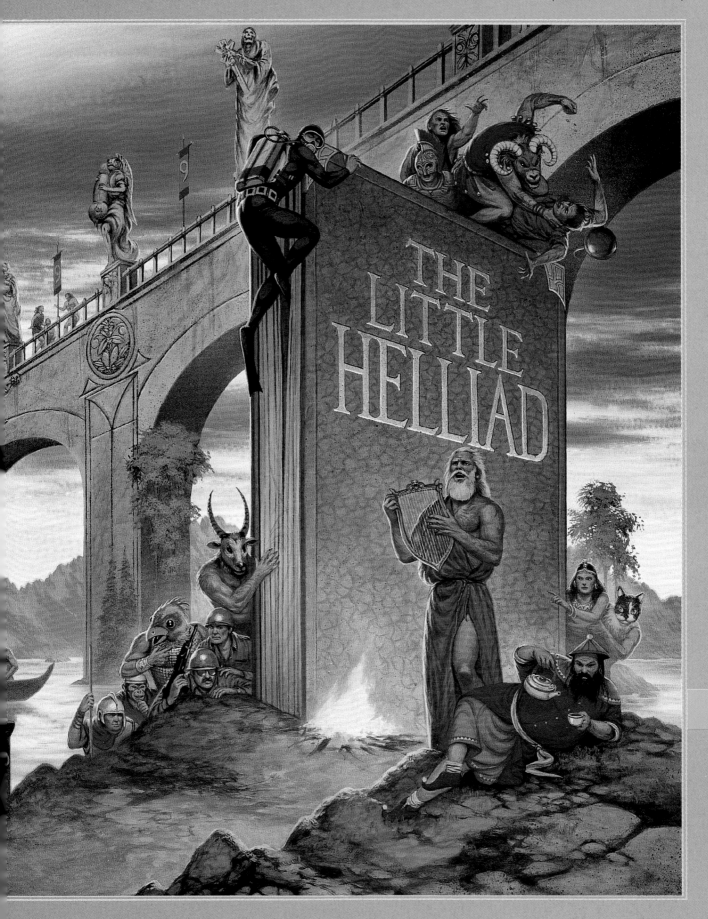

Time Gate
(Baen Books, 1989)

Time Gate is for an anthology by Robert Silverberg about a computer that can create extremely detailed and lifelike constructs of historical personalities. Ultimately, some of the computer-generated people want to break out of the confines of the digital environment, and I represented this with Joan of Arc smashing the computer with her sword.

The sketch for *Saint Joan and the Computer* was done for the *Time Gate* book, but the publisher opted to go with the idea above. I thought the rejected idea was so good that I sent the sketch to *Amazing Stories* as prospective cover art. Happily, they shared my enthusiasm for the idea, and commissioned it for their magazine.

Saint Joan and the Computer has a lot of meaning for me because it expresses my love/hate relationship with the computer. I am pleased with all the computer can do, but for me as an artist, it was a bit like opening Pandora's box. Mastering new software can be time consuming and frustrating, a lot of manuals are incomprehensible, and sometimes technical issues get in the way of making art. When the computer crashes unexpectedly, irretrievably erasing hours of work, I really do want to put all my computer equipment on top of a bonfire and light the match myself.

Finding the right computer for this painting was a challenge. I initially thought I would use a Cray supercomputer, but when I got pictures from the Cray Company, they looked less like computers than giant garbage dumpsters with a few flashing lights. Accuracy is great, but in this instance, I didn't think most people would get what they were. 'Oh look, Joan of Arc is burning a garbage bin!' I finally found the reference I needed in the 1960s movie *Charlie*, with Cliff Robertson. The computers in the film were not state-of-the-art, in fact, they were so old they still used tape drives. Nevertheless, they look like computers to the average person, and that's what I needed.

I am constantly recruiting friends and family members as models – they work for nothing! I have an extensive costume closet for just such occasions. Over the years, I've collected period clothing, space suits, swords, ray guns and monster masks. As my wife tells our friends, 'Every night is like Hallowe'en.' The model for the monk on the left-hand side, lighting the fire, is Michael Lloyd, a fine matte artist I worked with at Disney, who made the mistake of staying with us while I was working on the painting.

Firetime
(Baen Books, 1984)

Both *Firetime* and *The Moon Goddess and the Son* were done for Jim Baen, owner and publisher of Baen Books. *Firetime* was the image Jim selected for the promotional materials announcing the start of his own line.

I started working with Baen when I first moved to New York, and after 12 years of continuous work, he is my longest professional association in this field. Publishing is a business where people move around a lot: editors come and go, art directors switch around as well, but Jim Baen remains a fixture in the industry.

I consider working with Jim one of my most productive professional relationships. Jim is willing to try new things, and let me execute ideas that other companies would have rejected as too unusual. Instances of breaking the rules are: the type running through the middle of the figures in *The King of Ys* series (see page 116), and the multi-figured Hieronymus Bosch inspired layouts for the *Hell* series (see page 108). He also was the first publisher to let me do a cover entirely on the computer, *Years of the City* (see page 85).

Baen definitely has creative input, however. He likes to mull over ideas when I deliver sketches, often making suggestions or revisions. More often than not, his ideas are good.

However, if I think a change will not work, I will explain why, and thrashing it out, we will come up with a mutually acceptable alternative. I don't always have this give-and-take at other companies; my opinions overruled, I've had to grin and bear it, even when I know a change is going to diminish the painting.

Baen has a reputation for being tough, and can be brusque at times, but personally, I like his forthrightness. You always know what he really thinks.

I did *American Gothic 3000* (see page 114), after seeing a retrospective of American Artist Grant Wood's work at the Whitney Museum of American Art in New York. The original of *American Gothic* was on display, and I found the painting surprising in several ways. It was smaller than I expected, but gemlike in its execution. The paint application was clean and exact, in perfect harmony with its upright, middle American subject. There were many small details in the piece that I had never noticed in reproduction, like the funny selection of plants on the porch, or the beautifully painted curtains in the upstairs window. It was another example of how seeing the original of a painting is so much more informative than seeing a reproduction.

American Gothic 3000 *(The Perseus Breed)*
(Pageant Books, 1987)

Starship and Haiku
(Del Rey Books, 1988)

Sky Road
(Del Rey Books, 1992)

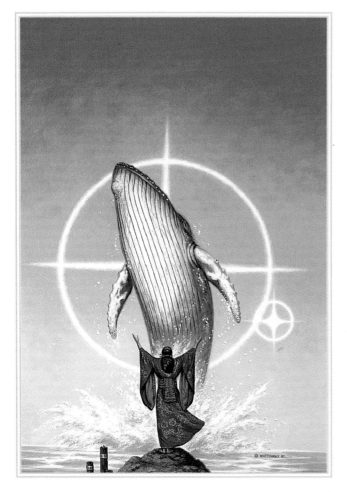

Showboat World
(DAW Books, 1980)

The Startling Worlds of Henry Kuttner
(Questar Books, 1986)

The King of Ys: Gallicenae
(Baen Books, 1987)

The model for *The King of Ys: Roma Mater* is my first wife, Barbara. I did these two pictures while we were getting divorced, and dealing with the dissolution of my ten year marriage in allegorical form was enormously therapeutic. I was able to explore my feelings, while giving concrete form to the issues behind the break up.

In the first picture, *King of Ys: Roma Mater*, Barb is in the foreground, holding a key that represents my emotional centre, or heart. In the background is a Roman soldier with a sword and shield, fighting a battle. The Roman is a surrogate for me, and the arrangement illustrates the main problem we had in the marriage; I worked too much and didn't give our relationship the time it needed.

In the second picture, *King of Ys: Gallicenae*, my metaphorical equivalent has moved to the foreground, and I now have the key in my hands. The key is an important symbol in these two paintings. I felt that if I was going to learn from the mistakes I made with Barb, I needed to rethink my life and complement work with other commitments. The switching of the key from Barb's hands to my own is symbolic of taking control of my destiny. Barb is now the background figure, holding a baby in her arms. She wanted kids, and I didn't, so I gave her a child in this picture, hoping that she would find what she wanted with someone else. Barb is now happily remarried, and a stepmother.

Yaril's Children
(Del Rey Books, 1987)

With rare exception I retain the rights to my original cover paintings. In fact, in my entire career, I can only think of two dozen instances where I have sold all rights to a piece, generally because the covers use copyrighted properties, such as Indiana Jones, Star Wars or Star Trek.

There are several secondary markets for science fiction and fantasy cover art. I have an agent in Germany who sells second rights to my covers to European and Japanese publishers. In overseas publishing, there seems to be less of an effort made to fit the cover art to the book's content, which results in some odd match ups. I observed this personally while visiting with best-selling author David Brin. A French-language version of one of his books had just been issued, and he was complaining that the cover had nothing to do with his story line. When he pulled the book out of his bag, I was shocked to discover that the cover featured one of my paintings. We both laughed as I explained that my German agent had sold the cover, which was originally done for another author's book. The art work was very specific to the original novel, and even at a stretch, bore no resemblance to Brin's book.

I've also sold finished works to game packagers, advertising firms and for use on trading cards. Additionally, there are art collectors who purchase science fiction and fantasy paintings for their personal enjoyment. At many of the larger science fiction conventions, art and poster sales are brisk. However, certain subjects work better than others as wall art. Covers tied to plots tend to be less popular then pretty images free of a narrative element. It is also true that fantasy art, like the two paintings featured here, *Yarril's Children* and *Seeking the Dream Brother*, are more saleable as collectible art than hard science fiction. Judging by art sales at science fiction conventions, the optimal composition would feature a beautiful, scantily clad female astride a unicorn with a cat perched on her shoulder. The background would contain a dragon and a castle, and in the clouds, Mr Spock's likeness.

My work is represented by Worlds Of Wonder in Washington, DC, headed by Jane Frank, a longtime collector of science fiction and fantasy art who turned her passion into a business. Jane has employed innovative marketing techniques, such as videos, specialized colour catalogues and even computer screen savers of her artists' work.

The Skeleton Bridge (see page 120), and *Killer* (see page 121), are heroic fantasy pieces. *Killer* shows the heavy influence of Frazetta, with his trademark triangular composition.

Seeking the Dream Brother
(Del Rey Books, 1988)

The Skeleton Bridge
(Marvel Comics, 1985)

Killer
(Baen Books, 1984)

TECHNIQUE

I have tried many different ways of working, and experimented with various mediums since I began painting, but this is a description of how I routinely approach a project.

When doing a book cover, I always read the entire manuscript through twice. The first time I read for pleasure, neither taking notes nor making sketches, but keeping an eye out for the main themes. I end up with a general impression of the book and how the cover might be handled. The second reading of the manuscript is one of professional scrutiny, an inventorying of interesting details and visual elements. As an illustrator, I strive to stay faithful to the spirit of a book, but my overriding concern is to create a compelling cover. After all, the purpose of book art is to snag the attention of the prospective reader – to get him or her to pick up the book. If something on my cover violates the author's narrative, it is either done for editorial or marketing reasons. Some books are less visual than others. At times, it is necessary to combine elements from various scenes, or add elements to spice up the situation. Here is an example: An astrophysicist, who also is a gifted science fiction writer, created a spaceship in one of his books that was based on hard science; if strictly followed, it would have looked like a flying coffee can. I used poetic licence and made it a more interesting vessel.

After reading the book, I make scores of thumbnail sketches, 2 x 3 in (5 x 7.5 cm) pencil doodles of the scenes and actions. When I have several I like, I open my paint box and re-do the more promising thumbnails in colour. Once I've worked out the overall colour solution for the top three or four ideas, I prepare final sketches for submission to the publisher. I do these the size of a printed book cover, 4 x 7 in (10 x 18 cm), and use gouache on illustration board. Gouache has several advantages at this stage: the medium is easy to correct, and has vibrant colours. I work straight from my head, without reference or models, so the sketches are fresh and direct, not limited by what reference I can find. I try to allow five or six days for the sketch stage, which is almost as long as it takes to do the final painting. Why do I allocate this much time? Because getting the right solution is critical to the success of the project. I like having the time to let ideas percolate in my mind, and the luxury to try scenes from different angles. I think shorting oneself on the conceptual side is a prescription for doing inferior work. A bad idea, no matter how beautifully rendered, is still a bad idea.

My studio This is my drawing board and palette, with the painting clipped to the board. I have reference all around, and stereo equipment on my right hand to provide entertainment.

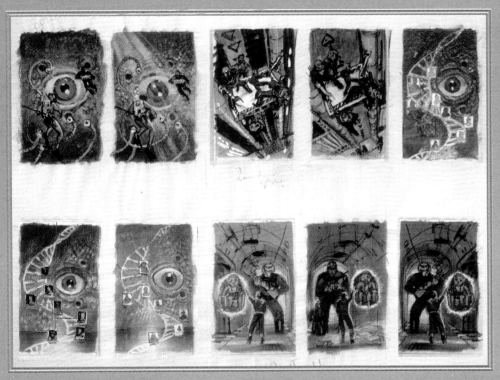

Thumbnail sketches
Each one is 2 x 3 in (5 x 7.5 cm), and done in gouache. These are the colour ideas I work up after doing many pages of rough pencil scribbles.

Final sketches These are the sketches I submitted to the art director for the book *Shapers* by Robert R. Chase (see the final on page 69). They are 4 x 7 in (10 x 18 cm), and painted in gouache. On all projects, I like to give the art director a variety of approaches using different angles and compositional solutions. Sketch 1, which was chosen for the final, was my favourite. Sketch 2 has an unusual down angle with vertical three-point perspective to vary the point of view. Sketch 3 is a montage approach, using the same big monster eye as sketch 1, with portraits of various characters on top of a DNA spiral. I did sketch 4, definitely the weakest idea, thinking the big-headed guy in the floating chair would be interesting, but it just looks silly.

Gallery of sketches When I turn in sketches on a project, I often wonder why one idea was chosen over another, and wish I had a chance to do an idea that was passed over. This is a diverse set of unused sketches for projects in this book. I work from my head, without much reference when doing sketches, so there is a freshness that is sometimes lost in a final painting. The finals always have much more detail, but sketches can be enjoyed as the original conception of the artist.

Yaril's Children
Final painting, page 118

The Armageddon Inheritance
Final painting, page 54

Harpy High
Final painting, page 37

Company Man
Final painting, page 62

At the Earth's Core
Final painting, page 24

The Wizard of Sunset Strip
Final painting, page 72

The Black Throne
Final painting, pages 70-1

The Black Throne
Final painting, pages 70-1

Sketch for **The Subway Wizard** – with the consent of the client, I changed quite a few details, including taking out the living broomstick and making the background more colourful.

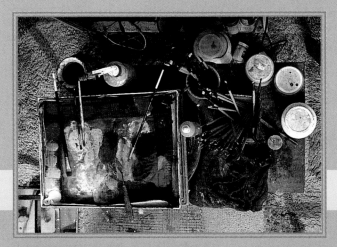

Reference photos for **The Subway Wizard**. Photo 1 is a proof sheet from my model shoot. Photo 2 is an 8 x 10 in blow up from the proofs. Photo 3 is a shot I took in a subway car.

When doing the final painting, I work three times up, so the actual painting is 14 x 22 in (35 x 56.5cm) for a front cover, and 22 x 30 in (56 x 76cm) for a wrap around. Using an opaque projector, I trace down the approved sketch to this size. This becomes my 'blueprint,' which assures both me and the art director that the approved design will be executed as approved. Next, I tighten up the drawing, get the reference I need and shoot models. For lead figures, I often hire models from the big Manhatten agencies and shoot with a professional photographer. I have a good photography set-up in my studio, and about half the time I shoot my own reference. I also recruit friends and family members to pose.

After transferring the drawing on to a canvas board, prepared with three coats of gesso and sanded, I start painting in acrylic. Acrylic is not as bright or direct as gouache, but achieves beautiful glazes, and I find it easier to get smooth skin tones and realistic modelling. I try to block in all the big areas of the painting before I get too involved with detail, and usually save the tight rendering for the last step – the 'polishing', so to speak. If I get stuck on a project, however, I often keep the momentum going by completely finishing the areas I'm sure of, and then tackling the trouble spots. In general, staying loose during the early stages of a project is the best way to paint.

The Artist's palette
This is looking down on my palette. I use a sealable plastic container that I cover with 2 sheets of vellum and keep wet all the time so my paint never dries on the palette.

125

Drawing Done on tracing paper, it flips back and forth over the painting as I work.

Painting day 1 (AM) Blocked in some basic background tones, getting rid of the white.

Painting day 1 (PM) All the dreaded white is gone, and the central focus established.

Painting day 2 Put in the midtone colours of the background people.

Painting day 3 Set up more background details, and started on the ceiling.

Painting day 6 Things are slowing down as I work on the background figure detail.

Painting day 9 Lots more detail put in, and I decide to lighten the wizard's robe.

Painting day 11 Painted the subway advertisements, filled with inside jokes.

Painting day 15 Did all the finishing touches, unifying and clarifying the whole composition.

The Subway Wizard Final painting. I am in the brown jacket on the left and my mother is the white-haired lady on the right. The rest of the people were inspired from reference shots taken in the subway. Can you recognize some of my paintings in the subway advertisements?

ENDINGS

I want to thank several people who helped with this book. My wife Cathleen for editing the book and trying to make me sound intelligent. Let me assure you, any bad stuff that remains is my fault. Friend Roberta Ludlow for reviewing the design throughout, and enduring endless questions about Quark XPress. Paul Chadwick for giving me some suggestions early on that influenced the look of the whole book. My big brother John for copy-editing and helping with grammar questions. By the way, I still don't have a clue what a split infinitive is.